CBT FOR DEPRESSION

CONNOR WHITELEY

No part of this book may be reproduced in any form or by any electronic or mechanical means. Including information storage, and retrieval systems, without written permission from the author except for the use of brief quotations in a book review.

This book is NOT legal, professional, medical, financial or any type of official advice.

Any questions about the book, rights licensing, or to contact the author, please email connorwhiteley@connorwhiteley.net

Copyright © 2024 CONNOR WHITELEY

All rights reserved.

DEDICATION
Thank you to all my readers without you I couldn't do what I love.

INTRODUCTION

Depression and other mood disorders are very common with the vast, vast majority of people having a good knowledge of what they are. Yet as psychology students and professionals, we know the causes and a wide range of treatments that are used to treat depression amongst other mood disorders.

But how does CBT work?

Or if you think you know the answer to that, do you know how CBT works from start to finish and the techniques that are involved in this very effective psychotherapy?

<u>What Does This Book Cover?</u>

If you want to learn about Cognitive Behavioural Therapy and mood disorders then this really is the book for you because this book covers the following:

- What are mood disorders?
- What is CBT?
- How does a CBT assessment work?

- What Cognitive Interventions Are Used In CBT?
- And so much more…

This book explores a wide range of CBT topics from how it works because of the theory behind it, to what's involved at the start and finish to what cognitive interventions are done in-between to actually decrease a person's psychological distress and improve their lives.

If you want a fun, engaging, easy-to-understand book with a conversational tone then this is definitely the book for you.

Who Is This Book For?

Like all of my books, this great book is written for psychology students and professionals wanting to learn more about CBT for depression and other mood disorders. It's okay if you have some knowledge about the topic and you want to learn more or if you know nothing about the topic.

You'll learn a lot in this brilliant book about CBT, how it works and mood disorders.

Bonus

This book includes a 3,000-word bonus critical review helping you to understand CBT at a much deeper level so you can learn about its flaws, advantages and theories behind it.

Who Am I?

Personally, I always love to know who the author is of the nonfiction I read so I know the information is coming from a good source. In case you're like me,

I'm Connor Whiteley, the internationally bestselling author of over 40 psychology books.

In addition, I am the host of *The Psychology World Podcast,* a weekly show exploring a new psychology topic each week and delivering the latest psychology news. Available on all major podcast apps and YouTube.

Finally, I am a psychology graduate studying a Clinical Psychology Masters at the University of Kent, England.

So now we know more about each other, let's dive into the great topic of mood disorders and CBT.

INTRODUCTION TO MOOD DISORDERS AND DEPRESSION

To make sure everyone is on the exact same page when it comes to Mood Disorders, I really want to spend the first two chapters of the book investigating these conditions in a bit more depth. Since it is impossible for us to understand how Cognitive Behavioral Therapy (CBT) is used to treat Mood Disorders if we simply don't know what they are.

As a result, mood disorders are a group of mental health conditions where there is a disturbance in mood and it is this disturbance that is hypothesized to be the main underlying feature of this condition.

In addition, there are two groups of mood disorders, and these groups are based on whether a person ever experiences a manic or hypomanic episode. This is where there are depressive (hypomanic) and bipolar (manic) disorders.

<u>What Is Major Depressive Disorder?</u>

Major Depressive or Depression Disorder (MDD) is the full name for the condition when a person says they have depression, so now we're looking at the diagnostic criteria for MDD because you can learn a lot about a condition through it.

For example, for a person to get a diagnosis of MDD they have to have five or more of the following symptoms at the same time during the same two-week period (we'll look at the 5 symptoms in a moment), and these symptoms have to represent a change from the person's normal functioning.

But one of the symptoms HAS to be either:
- Depressed mood
- Loss of interest or pleasure

And if you've studied depression before then you can understand why, because a depressed mood and a loss of interest or pleasure in activities that the person used to find pleasurable is flat out critical and so common for a diagnosis.

As well as these symptoms have to cause the person clinically significant distress or impairs their functioning in the social, job and other areas of their life.

Furthermore, for a diagnosis, a person must have at least 5 of these symptoms as mentioned earlier:
- A stark diminished interest or pleasure in most, almost all or all activities most of the day nearly every day.
- A depressed mood for most of the day nearly every day.

And a depressed mood includes a person feeling sad, empty, hopeless and more.
- Hypersomnia or insomnia nearly every day

In other words, struggling to get to sleep or sleeping a lot every day.
- Significant weight loss or gain when the person isn't dieting.

- Experiencing loss of energy or fatigue nearly every day
- Experiencing psychomotor agitation or retardation nearly every day.
- Having a diminished ability to concentrate or think or being indecisive nearly every day.
- Feelings of worthlessness or excessive or inappropriate guilt.
- Recurrent thoughts of death recurrent, suicidal ideation without a specific plan or a suicide attempt or a specific plan.

Also that's another reason why it is so important to talk and learn about depression because it is a major factor in suicide, so it's critical that depression is treated. If you want to learn more about suicide then please check out my book Suicide Psychology.

How Is Depression Treated?

Now that we have a basic understanding of MDD, and this understanding is expanded in the critical review at the back of the book, we now need to know how MDD is treated.

Whilst I don't know about other countries, but I strongly imagine they have something similar, the UK has the National Institute For Health and Care Excellence (NICE) and they examine all the published and unpublished research to produce guidelines about treatments for conditions. Therefore, only the best, most evidence-based treatments get recommended in NICE.

We'll use this resource now to look at MDD.

According to NICE (2009), when it comes to subthreshold and mild to moderate depression, the best treatments are low-intensity psychological interventions, individual guided self-help based on CBT, group CBT (this involves between 10 and 12 meetings), computerized CBT as well as a structured group physical activity programme.

However, if anyone doesn't want CBT then there are other options for them. For example, they could have behavioural activation (something we'll look at later), Interpersonal Psychotherapy, behavioural couples therapy, counselling or short-term psychodynamic therapy.

Personally, I think I would always hope someone goes for CBT because it is the most evidence-based, effective and "easiest" to both administer and potentially do. Even though we all know how difficult therapy can be on the client and therapy only works if the client puts in the work.

The old saying "you get out what you put in" seriously applies to therapy.

Moreover, when it comes to moderate to severe depression, NICE (2009) recommends a combination of anti-depressants and high-intensity CBT or Interpersonal Psychotherapy.

The CBT involves (well, according to NICE), 16 to 20 sessions over 3 to 4 months and this includes two sessions a week for the first 2 to 3 weeks and there are follow-up sessions after the therapy over the following 3 to 4 months.

However, at least in the UK with our medical care thankfully being free at the time of writing, this does not happen. I cannot remember the last clinical psychologist I spoke to that said they gave 16, let alone 20 sessions of CBT and I have never heard of follow-up sessions.

Again, this is the interesting problem and conflict

between what the research says and what's practical with public health budgets and other real-world factors.

Additionally, when it comes to Interpersonal Psychotherapy, this is similar to CBT in the sense that it involves 16 to 20 sessions over a course of 3 to 4 months.

Finally, when it comes to complex and severe depression, so the complex part might come from a comorbidity and the person might have depression *and* another mental health condition, like a type of anxiety disorder.

When a therapist needs to treat a client with complex and severe depression, NICE (2009) recommends they've referred to specialist mental health teams (definitely) and if you're read my *Working With Children and Young People* clinical psychology book then this is where Tier 4 CAMHS services would get involved.

Moreover, the mental health team should assess the client's risk of self-harming, they would assess the client's psychological stressors, personality factors, relationship difficulties as well but also for co-morbidities. Such as, alcohol and substance misuse and personality disorders.

That information that the mental health team gathers for the psychologist is absolutely critical in helping to treat the complex and severe depression.

Now we understand one type of mood disorder, what makes bipolar disorder different?

INTRODUCTION TO BIPOLAR DISORDER

Since the entire purpose of this book is to focus on the psychological treatments available for depression, these first two chapters really are just to get everyone on the same page and give you a basic understanding of these mental health conditions. Therefore, if you want to learn more and go more in-depth into the causes and non-psychological treatments for these conditions, please check *Abnormal Psychology: The Causes And Treatments for Depression, Anxiety And More*.

Anyway, you have depressive disorders where a person lacks energy and is hypomanic, but you also have mood disorders that give people energy and makes them experience manic episodes. Therefore, this group of mood disorders are called bipolar and Related Disorders as well as these include the following:

- Bipolar Type 1 Disorder
- Bipolar Type 2 Disorder
- Cyclothymic Disorder

- Substance or Medication-Induced Bipolar and Related Disorder
- Bipolar and Related Disorder because of another Medical Condition
- Other Specified Bipolar and Related Disorder
- Unspecified Bipolar and Related Disorder

<u>What Is Bipolar Disorder?</u>

Bipolar disorder is when a person experiences both depressive periods and manic periods that can last hours, days, week or even months. Also, during the depressive or "low" periods, a person's symptoms can include:

- Loss of energy
- Sadness
- Difficulty concentrating
- Loss of enjoyment from things they once found pleasurable
- Feelings of worthlessness or hopelessness
- Uncontrollable crying
- Irritability
- Difficulty concentrating
- Insomnia or hypersomnia
- Difficulty making decisions
- A change in appetite causing weight loss or gain
- Thoughts of death or suicide

As you can see in relation to the depressive episode, there is no difference at all between depression and bipolar disorder but the difference comes from a person's symptoms of mania or the "highs". These symptoms include:

- Rapid speech

- Poor concentration
- Excessive excitement, hopefulness and happiness
- Sudden changes in mood from being joyful to being hostile, angry and irritable
- Restlessness
- High sex drive
- Increased energy and less need for sleep
- Tendency to make grand, unattainable plans
- Tendency to poor judgement. Like deciding to quit their job.
- Increased impulsivity
- Drug and alcohol abuse

Overall, now we know more about mood disorders, we can start to understand how they're treated because that is a critical thing to understand.

WHAT IS THE COGNITIVE APPROACH TO DEPRESSION?

Moving onto the next section of the book, this has to be one of the most interesting *"causes"* chapters because it seems that depression is mainly caused by cognitive factors, and if anyone still believes the rubbish biological explanations for depression that has been very disproved at this point, please read Read and Moncrieff (2022) it is a fantastic paper. And I have never ever said that about an academic paper before, so believe me it is good.

What Is The Cognitive Approach To Depression?

Anyway, according to the findings of Westbrook, Kennerley & Kirk (2011), there is a lot of evidence that shows that a lot of psychological conditions are associated with a range of cognitive factors. For instance, mental health conditions can be caused by negative thoughts and beliefs, information processing biases and dysfunctional ways of thinking.

As well as if you read *Abnormal Psychology: The*

Causes and Treatments For Depression, Anxiety And More, you'll see the full range of causes for Major Depression Disorder.

Moreover, the first people to pioneer the cognitive approach or explanation for depression were Albert Ellis (1962) and Aaron Beck (1967). Due to they saw that psychopathology (a very old term in all fairness) was caused by a person developing biased information processing, irrational beliefs and dysfunctional ways of thinking.

In addition, the core principle of this approach is that our emotions and behaviour (like the manifested symptoms of depression) are strongly influenced by our mental processes, like our beliefs, thoughts and interpretations.

Speaking of interpretations, this refers to how two people can experience the exact same event but react differently depending on their interpretation, and this doesn't necessarily have to directly lead to a particular emotion, like a depressed state.

This is important to remember because this is a key concept of CBT because CBT pays attention to a client's behavioural responses and their biased attentional processes, since these can serve to accidentally maintain unhelpful beliefs, and prevent the client disconfirming these inaccurate beliefs. Instead strengthening and even magnifying them.

Overall, creating a vicious cycle.

Furthermore, the cognitive approach is important in treatment because it believes by helping a client to develop alternative perspectives on their experiences, this can reduce their psychological distress, and this change in perspective can be achieved through verbal and behavioural methods.

In other words, this can be achieved through talking therapy, cognitive interventions and behavioural activation.

Again, we'll have chapters on all of these later on.

Lastly for this section, as this is serving as a short introduction to CBT, CBT is a broad movement within psychotherapies as CBT isn't a single therapy. Especially when you start to consider "second" and "third wave" CBTs, with third wave therapies focusing on the meta-cognitive level and helping clients to become more aware of their own thoughts and feelings.

What Are Levels Of Cognition?

For the rest of the chapter, we do need to look at the most important aspects of the cognitive approach since a person's levels of cognition is such a foundation part of CBT and it is something we will draw on more and more throughout the book.

Therefore, the levels of cognitions are:

- Automatic Thoughts
- Immediate Beliefs- involving rules, attitudes and assumptions a person about the self and world.
- Core Beliefs

Negative Automatic Thoughts

This is the first level of a person's cognition because automatic thoughts are thoughts that just happen automatically without the person putting any effort into them. Although, it does take a little bit of effort to pay attention and notice them.

Additionally, these automatic thoughts are specific thoughts about particular situations with them being brief and common, so a person might not be fully aware of them.

The reason why these automatic thoughts are so important in therapy and mental health conditions is that people often perceive these thoughts as believable and taken as accurate especially when their emotions are strong, with them possibly taking the form of images of themselves or others or just thoughts.

However, whilst we'll look at some examples in a moment of automatic thoughts that depressed people have, these thoughts can or easily can become conscious. Allowing a person to detect them and think about how accurate they are. That's one of the aims of CBT.

Examples of Negative Automatic Thoughts Include:

- I'm worthless
- I'm useless
- I shouldn't be alive
- I shouldn't burden people
- I hate myself
- The world is better off without me

<u>Dysfunctional Assumptions</u>

These assumptions are often seen as the link between a person's core beliefs and their Negative Automatic Thoughts, at least in depression, and these are basically a person's rules for living. As well as they often consist of conditional propositions of "if… then" statements.

For example, as a non-depressed person, I might think "if I go to university and see my friends then I will have a good time". Yet as you'll see later this isn't how a depressed person could think.

Subsequently, because these assumptions are a deeper level of cognition than automatic thoughts then they aren't as directly obvious as them. Therefore, it's perfectly possible that they aren't easy to verbalise and they frequently need to be inferred from a person's actions and behaviours.

Also, these assumptions could be culturally reinforced and may be approved of in certain cultures, but not in others so that is always something to bear in mind when we encounter CBT, or any psychotherapy to be honest.

Nonetheless, these assumptions become problematic and dysfunctional when they become overly-too rigid and over-generalised with them typically being addressed later on in the therapy.

Since it is also important to note in CBT, you do have to work in order of the levels of cognition, you cannot work on a person's core beliefs or assumptions without tackling automatic thoughts for example. Or you could, it just wouldn't end well and there's a much higher chance of the therapy failing than succeeding and that isn't what we want in the slightest.

<u>Core Beliefs</u>

The final, deepest level of a person's cognition is their core beliefs and these entail their most fundamental beliefs about the self, others and the world in general. Therefore, these are flat out not immediately accessible to our consciousness except in very rare instances.

Also, these are fairly stable beliefs that are hard to change but not impossible, and they might make up general and absolute statements. For example, if a person says "I'm a bad person".

Typically, these are learnt in early life because of childhood experiences, but they could develop later because of traumatic experiences, for instance.

Due to them not being available to our consciousness, we typically cannot tackle them directly in short-term therapy for conditions like depression and anxiety. Yet we can get to them indirectly.

As a result, once a core belief has formed, information is interpreted through the lens of these beliefs and these beliefs can be healthy and adaptive for a person, or unhealthy and maladaptive. And as you can imagine, after one of these unhealthy beliefs have "activated" then so do the dysfunctional assumptions and negative thoughts.

Core Belief Examples From Depression

If someone has a core belief of "I am useless" then this is how it affects the rest of their cognition. It would affect their assumptions because they will live their life believing if they try anything new then they will fail and if they don't try their hardest then they will fail.

In addition, they will live their life by believing that in order for them to be good enough, they have to succeed in everything they do and they have to try harder than everyone else as well.

Another core belief is that if a person says "I am unlovable" then they will have the assumption of if they let themselves care about anyone then they will get hurt, and if they allow people to get to know them then they will leave them.

Resulting in them living their life with the idea that to be lovable, they must be in a relationship to be lovable and they need to put the needs of others ahead of their own. As well as in order to be safe they need to keep themselves to themselves.

And as you can see with this example in particular, if someone has this set of beliefs then their avoidance and safety behaviours will be very maladaptive. Since if you believe the best way to live is to be in a relationship and put the needs of others ahead of you. Then you will be very clingy and needy to some extent, and that can cause relationship problems creating a self-fulfilling prophecy of people leaving you.

Also if you believe people will leave you so you avoid people getting hurt. Then you'll be lonely and suffer all the negative mental health outcomes associated with it.

Thinking Errors/Biases

If you've studied depression before then you might be familiar with this section of the chapter because there are a lot of commonalities between all types of CBT (at least "first-wave" therapies) and the types of cognitive biases and errors a CBT therapist would encounter. Therefore, here are the following cognitive errors a therapist is likely to encounter and I have broken them up so you can clearly see the error and an example of what it is like:

- All or nothing- if I can't be good at art then I'm useless at all school subjects.

- Exaggerated standards/expectations- if I can't past a driving test then I'm a failure
- Catastrophising- if I ask a guy out and he rejects me then I'm unlovable and it's the end of my life.

- Selective attention to the negative/threat- I'm useless because I failed English but I got A* in all my other subjects.
- Over-generalising- I hit that one curve on my driving test so I'm going to hit all curves and I'm never going to pass.
- Dismissing the positive- I might have passed all school subjects, have a lot of friends but they don't matter because I'm useless at driving.

- Magnifying/minimising- minimising the positive and magnifying the bad
- Jumping to conclusions
- Emotional reasoning- being irrational and basing your reason on emotion, not fact.
- Personalising
- Internalising/externalising

So now we understand how depression is caused by psychological factors, how does the behavioural approach see depression and its causes?

WHAT IS THE BEHAVIOURAL PRINCIPLE FOR DEPRESSION?

After looking at the *Cognitive* aspect of *C*BT, we now need to look at the behavioural aspect because you cannot have the cognitive aspect without the behavioural and vice versa for CBT. Since it is the combination of both parts that makes CBT so powerful and beneficial to our clients.

Therefore, the behavioural principle is built on the assumption that what we do has a powerful influence in maintaining or changing our how think and feel about certain experiences. As well as by trying out different and new behavioural responses then a client can make big changes to their thinking and feelings. In CBT this is done through behavioural experiments and is called behavioural activation.

<u>What Is The Role Of Avoidance And Safety behaviours?</u>

Now if you've read my <u>*CBT For Anxiety*</u> book, then you know that I love talking about safety behaviours because they are the biggest con we could ever hope to pull on ourselves and they are absolutely fascinating to me.

Since safety behaviours are, well, behaviours that are a core factor in maintaining but also changing our psychological beliefs and states. Since these are behaviours that we use as responses to negative cognitions and experiences that might have a significant effect on whether the emotion persists.

For example, I know this isn't depression related but safety behaviours are a lot easier to see in anxious people so I want to use one for teaching purposes.

When a person with Social Anxiety Disorder has to face a social situation, they get anxious and fearful and they *believe* they're going to shake violently like an earthquake and they're going to be as red as a tomato. Therefore, to counteract this, an anxious person might grip a water bottle so they don't shake as much and they avoid eye contact to help them with their nerves.

But after behavioural experiments (there's an entire chapter looking at this later on), the person realizes that their safety behaviours make them worse and look *more* anxious to the person they're talking to.

This is why I think safety behaviours are such cons because we truly believe safety behaviours help us and without them clients basically think they will die, but in reality it is our safety behaviours that don't help us at all.

And as a more psychological way to say this is that whilst safety behaviours are intended to protect us from threat or prevent harm, they may reduce our anxiety in the short term yet they always have unintended consequences about maintaining our anxiety in the longer term.

On the other hand, you have avoidance behaviours involving when a person completely avoids a situation, wants to escape a situation and if they find themselves in a situation then they engage in safety behaviours to make it "manageable". These are more relevant for anxiety disorders but avoidance behaviours still apply to depressive episodes as well.

What is The Behavioural Approach And Behavioural Therapy?

We already know what the behavioural approach is but now we need to see how it applies to therapy, leading to the creation of Behaviour Therapy by Wolpe (1958), with this therapy seeing that a lot of mental health conditions are the results of learnt reactions to life experiences.

Therefore, the behavioural approach looks at learning therapy to explain mental health conditions and for the 1950s, this was considered a more scientific and objective approach. Now, I say for the 1950s on purpose, because I flat out cannot see how this approach is very scientific by today's standards.

Also, I was reading the Read and Moncrieff paper yesterday as I write this and there's a stupid argument saying that we should never apply today's standards of science to 40 to 50 years ago. But that is stupid because all sciences need to be progressing, testing and developing their understanding always and if certain beliefs and findings have to be dropped because there isn't the evidence to support them then so be it.

If we ever want psychology to be a great science then everything we do has to be backed up by evidence.

Anyway, tangent over.

As a result, the behavioural approach believes that dysfunctional behaviours, the same goes for adaptive behaviours, can be acquired through learning. This involves two principles.

Firstly, this involves classical conditioning where a person learns an association between two stimuli, the conditioned stimulus that predicts the occurrence of the unconditioned stimulus.

Secondly, you have operant conditioning, which involves the person learning a specific behaviour or response and this behaviour leads to rewarding or reinforcing consequences. Also I will give examples in a moment to help apply this directly to depression.

Operant conditioning can lead to positive reinforcement and this is when a behaviour leads to the introduction of a desirable stimulus, so this rewards and maintains a mental health condition. An example could be when a person is in a depressed mood, they get attention from their parents, which is a wonderful luxury if the parents rarely give attention to the client.

Additionally, it leads to negative reinforcement where the behaviour leads to the removal of an aversive stimulus. For example, for a depressed person, whenever they're in a depressed mood they don't have to drive their sister to school and they hate the drive because it's awful. It's a fictional example totally but it demonstrates the point clearly.

Overall, both of these outcomes are rewarding to the client so this leads to an increase in how common and often these behaviours are used.

Equally, behaviours can lead to positive punishment, which is where the behaviour leads to an aversive stimulus being introduced, leading to a reduction in the frequency of the behaviour.

Also, negative punishment is an important concept too because this involves a behaviour followed by the removal of a positive stimulus so this cause the frequency of the behaviour to reduce.

Finally, you have extinction where the behaviour that had had previously been reinforced is no longer effective. For example, if the depressed mood no longer got the client attention, love and affection from their parents. Then it would no longer be an effective behaviour to meet those basic needs of the client.

Ultimately, learning theory can be used to explain how certain maladaptive or unhelpful behaviours develop and maintain mental health conditions by having positive or rewarding outcomes.

Another example is that classical conditioning is used to explain theories of the development of certain emotional disorders, like anxiety and depressive disorders. Whereas operant conditioning is often used to explain how a range of mental health difficulties develop and are maintained.

Both of these learning theories are critical in the development of important psychological treatments including behaviour modification and behaviour therapy.

Overall, if you take anything away from this chapter, let it be that the idea of the behavioural approach is that it is built on the idea that a person can unlearn their maladaptive emotions and behaviours.

INTRODUCTION TO CBT MODELS AND HOW CBT WORKS

Whilst this next chapter is more of a brief overview of the content we'll be investigating and examining in more depth in the rest of the book, I wanted to introduce the information here so we can ease into this great topic a little more.

<u>What Are The Generic CBT Models And Models Specific To Depression?</u>

When it comes to CBT, there is one main model that always springs to mind for me whenever I talk about it or learn about this topic, and that is the 5P Model of CBT. If you've done clinical psychology before then at this point I sort of liken it to seeing an old friend again, because the 5P model is always your friend and it will never leave you. But if you haven't done clinical psychology before then you are in for a treat.

The 5P model is based on the idea that a client has 5 factors or facets of their mental health condition that you can use to inform your formulation and then this in turn helps a therapist to decide what intervention to use. Or to be honest, how to make CBT a little more targeted for this particular client.

The five facets are:

- Presenting issues- focusing on the here and now
- Precipitating factors focusing on what triggered the condition recently
- Predisposing factors- focusing on things in the past
- Perpetuating factors- known as a vicious cycle or what maintains the condition
- Protective factors- a client's strengths and personal resources

Now even though, as therapists (future or current) we might not be interested at all at first in protective factors, this is a massive mistake because we need to see protective factors as things that are just as important as how the condition is manifesting. Since we can help our client to see how brilliant, strong and resilient they are by pointing out all their strengths and resources.

This is even more important when we consider how depression leads to biased cognitive processes that makes the person believe they are absolutely useless.

Which is a rather great segway into our Depression model of CBT.

The Longitudinal Model Of Depression

Of course, this model was created by the Grandfather of CBT and Depression himself Aaron Beck (1967, 1976) with the help of J Beck (1993) on the assumption that a client's early experience, core beliefs, rules and assumptions (how the client believes the world works) are responsible for depression. As well as critical incidents, how beliefs activate, Negative Automatic Thoughts and a client's feelings, behaviours and physiology also play a role.

Also, whilst this is a lot of information, this model is saying that depression isn't instant and it doesn't develop overnight. It takes several events and processes in a client's life to form the biased and negative cognitive processes that ultimately leads to maladaptive coping mechanisms that manifest because someone has depression.

Additionally, this model plays off Beck's Cognitive Triad for depression about a person's negative thoughts and beliefs about the self, others and the world and their faulty thinking processes.

Therefore, by using Beck's theories about the cognitive approaches for depression, we can modify "basic" or "general" CBT to become more targeted for depression.

How Does CBT Work?

It's all well and good me using the words CBT and explaining its effects and all that, but we need to know how it works as this helps to understand why it is effective and we can learn things about depression because of it.

As a result, CBT works by it helps clients to think about the role that their own interpretation plays in their experience of depression, and how this interpretation is maintained by their behaviours as well as emotions. This is where the psychoeducation component of CBT comes in.

Then CBT helps clients to learn alternative ways to interpret these experiences by learning cognitive strategies, and CBT helps a person to make changes to their situation by trying out new ways of understanding themselves, others and the world by using behavioural experiments.

That's a quick overview of CBT and this will most certainly be explored in greater depth in the following chapters.

What Are The Core Principles Of CBT?

Personally, it isn't only the evidence-based approach and sheer devotion to empirical rigour (to a large extent) that I love about CBT, it also its core principles that I really like too.

For example, CBT has to be a time-limited, structured, collaborative process between the therapist and the client so the client gets a say in how they are treated and that helps the therapeutic alliance.

In addition, in CBT, the therapist has to be active and directive to prevent large tangents, this is a major thing that separates it from psychodynamic models, but there is still enough freedom for the client to talk about things so CBT is more of a guided discovery process of their psychological distress.

Moreover, CBT is goal orientated and problem-focused, formulation driven and it isn't just a talking therapy, it is also a *doing* therapy.

That's something that I find interesting about people's perception of CBT and other "talking therapies". A lot of people believe that psychologists listen to people talk about their mental health difficulties when in reality, CBT is a LOT more involved than that.

Some of this doing involves behavioural experiments (more on that later) and in-vivo work as well as homework making the client do work outside the therapy session.

Finally, the last three core principles of CBT is

that there is a strong therapeutic alliance (and the client needs to feel safe), the therapy aims to help the client to become their own therapist so there is less chance of relapse after they leave therapy and CBT is empirical, so the theory and treatment needs to be evaluated at the end.

To be honest, it's these strong guiding core principles that really makes me like CBT because it so committed (like all psychotherapies really) to doing what is best for the client in an empirical way that it is hard not to like, respect and be rather passionate about it.

At least in my biased opinion, but the free bonus Critical Review at the back does highlight the problems with CBT.

WHAT STEPS ARE INVOLVED IN CBT?

Personally, I think whenever students set out to learn about a psychological therapy, regardless of whatever one it is (there are TONS after all), the problem we all face is that we learn about certain areas of the therapy and we don't see how all these sections work together to make a course of psychotherapy.

For example, if you think about CBT, we all learn about behavioural activation, challenging a person's cognitive beliefs and formulation. But how do these three things actually link together to form a course of psychotherapy?

That's exactly the question we'll answer in this chapter.

Therefore, when it comes to a course of CBT treatment, it always starts with the psychological assessment. This is a critical tool that is explored a lot more in the next few chapters because a lot of information is needed to give a therapist a good understanding about the client.

Secondly, a formulation is conducted and this is more information gathered with the client collaboratively to tailor make the therapy to what the client needs. This is also explored later on.

Thirdly, in "general" CBT, the client and therapist go through a discussion of alternative explanations for a mental health condition and explore theory A versus theory B.

For example, this is a lot easier to explain with anxiety so I'll use that. Since a client might believe with every fibre of their being that if they don't use their safety behaviour of clutching a water bottle for dear life, then they will shake so badly they will look like an idiot. That is Theory A.

Then the therapist could suggest that they don't shake as badly as they believe and they might look more personable, human and approachable if they don't use their safety behaviours. This is Theory B.

Overall, this third stage of CBT is largely done through behavioural experiments, behavioural activation and challenging their cognition beliefs. More on that later on.

A part of this third stage but this is also its own fourth stage is that the client works towards goals and creates their own list of goals (more on this in the Behavioural Activation Chapter).

As well as this leads directly into the fifth stage with specific treatment strategies. For example, now that the groundwork has been laid and the therapist knows enough about the client to have a very good idea about what will work and what won't. They can start working with the client to do cognitive restructuring, behavioural experiments and exposure and response prevention.

In addition, stage 5 might be focused on working with a client on a certain task of their mental health condition. For example, depression makes a person socially withdrawn so the therapist might work with them to help them return to a single friend that they've lost. If this works then the person now knows how to get a friend back, but this doesn't help them in all other areas of functioning that they experience clinically significant distress and impairment in.

This is where stage 6 comes in.

Due to stage 6 is all about generalizing the skills and techniques learnt in stage 5 to other areas of functioning, so the client knows how to use more adaptive coping mechanisms and they can start functioning again in other areas.

Penultimately, there will be some work on relapse prevention so the depression doesn't return to clinically significant levels after the therapy and the final stage is a follow-up later on to make sure everything is still okay for the client.

Moreover, supervision is constantly used in CBT because a therapist is always well prepared for the course of treatment through their supervision log with the client's latest measures, formulations and more included, and the basics are always covered (like I mentioned earlier by not overlooking or underestimating anything) and the formulation is always flexible and should be constantly evolving, changing and updating.

What's The Format Of CBT?

To recap and have all the information in one area, CBT can be delivered one-on-one or in groups, it's a highly structured as well as manualized psychotherapy and more client-formulation driven compared to other therapies.

In addition, CBT can be very specific to a certain

condition, like depression or one of the anxiety disorders, or it can be transdiagnostic. This is great if a client has two or more mental health conditions at the same time that need to be treated together.

However, what's really interesting and exciting and I do have a book on mHealth Apps coming out later in 2024, is that CBT is increasingly being offered in different formats. For instance, you have CBT being delivered over the phone and it can be offered by apps and games. As seen in Silver Cloud, a CBT app and game for adults with anxiety, depression or stress.

Another example is Pesky Gnats, a game designed for young people with anxiety and low mood.

Personally, I really doubt this area of development will slow down and this does represent us with a lot of exciting opportunities and a much greater need for research into this area.

But the future of psychotherapy and CBT is very, very exciting indeed.

INTRODUCTION TO CBT ASSESSMENT

Whilst we'll go into psychological and CBT assessments in even more depth in the next chapter, I certainly think this is a great, very interesting chapter that introduces you to a lot of great topics about assessment.

Since this chapter essentially sets out to answer one of the most important questions when a therapist meets a client, what goes into their psychological assessment?

That's a very important question we'll answer in this next chapter.

Therefore, when it comes to a client getting a psychological assessment, what generally happens is that they undergo an assessment plan where the therapist finds out the client's:

- Current mental health difficulties
- Presenting problems
- The history of their problems
- Any other problems they're having
- Their expectations

Personally, I do hate the term "problem" as do a

lot of clinical psychologists because that term is very blaming, negative and it isn't helping the client at all. Since mental health conditions aren't a client's fault, so why use blaming language?

Anyway, a client's expectations are very important here too because a lot of people still believe psychologists are just psychodynamic therapists so they lay down on a couch, talk about their problems and then at the end of the session, they're magically cured (Yes I know that isn't how psychodynamic therapy works too).

So in this assessment plan and initial conversation, setting expectations and the fact that they have to do work as well is very important.

In addition, a therapist would include any observations they make of the client in the plan, any of the client's personal history, formal measures (such as test results), practicalities and explanations for the difficulties too.

What's Mentioned In A Client's Current Presenting Problems?

When a therapist is working with a client to understand their current presenting problems, the therapist will investigate their symptoms, emotions, behaviour, thoughts and beliefs as well as anything physical.

Furthermore, a therapist would look at the severity of the symptoms too because that is important in giving a diagnosis, and they'll look at a client's triggers, modifiers and consequences of their behaviours (that's an important concept for later) as well as any patterns of recurrence and change.

Overall, the entire point of understanding a client's current presenting problems is for a therapist to understand what is the problem, where is it and when does it occur and most importantly, what is the impact of the problem on a person's life?

As we saw earlier, this question around impact is important, not only because of the diagnostic criteria from the DSM-5 but also you can start to understand what the client wants to work towards when it comes to setting goals (more on that later on with behavioural activation).

Finally for this section, a therapist would look at a client's maladaptive coping mechanisms for dealing with their mental health difficulties. Like staying in bed for long periods of time, not trying anything and avoiding people at all costs.

History Of Problem

When it comes to a therapist looking at the History part of the assessment, they'll ask questions like:

- When did the problem begin?
- How has it developed?
- Are there obvious precipitating factors (such as life events)?
- Are there any difficulties associated with the above?
- Are there other problems which are being experienced?
- Does the person have any medical or physical problems?

And when it comes to asking about substance use, this is a very tricky question to ask, because people could avoid answering it completely, or they can effectively flip out at the therapist because they're feeling accused.

For example, the last thing you ever want a client to believe is you, as the therapist, are labelling them a "druggie" just because they have a mental health condition. That really isn't going to help the therapeutic relationship form.

Therefore, what one of my lecturers does, is they stress how this is a standard question that they ask everyone, even when it actually isn't. This makes the question become less targeted at the client (in their eyes) and it makes the loaded question seem just like any other question they're been asking for a while.

Something as a, current or future, therapist would will need to be greatly aware of how you ask questions and how they can be misinterpreted.

How Is Risk Used In A Psychological Assessment?

When it comes to a psychological assessment, assessing a potential client for risk is very important because if a client is at high risk of suicide, self-harming or poses a risk to others, then they can effectively jump the queue and get earlier access to therapy. Due to these are the people that really need it.

As a result, a client's history, current intent and thoughts and goals are looked at. For example, do they desire treatment and what would they like to gain or change from treatment?

Current Life Circumstances

This is another good area to investigate during an assessment because you can ask about a client's home circumstances so you can see if there are any home problems that could be precipitating or maintaining factors. Or satisfactions that can be protective factors for the client.

The same goes for their employment situation

because we already know that unemployment and poverty are major predictors of mental health conditions, so by asking about their employment situation we can understand more about them.

Also, we can find out about their protective factors. For example, if they have aspirations and love their job then these are two major areas of protective factors.

Additionally, when I was talking to a lecturer once they were discussing about something the reasons that suicidal people have to live can be very, very simple to you and me but actually they're important reasons to them. The lecturer was once working with a suicidal woman and her reasoning for staying alive just a little longer was that she wanted to watch the latest series of her favourite programme. And thankfully for the therapy, the new season wasn't out for a little while.

In other words, do not underestimate the power of anything in therapy even if it is as simply as a client enjoys work because they get to talk to clients. That's a simple reason but it is another protective factor potentially.

<u>Other interests</u>

A client's other interests are typically asked about in an assessment, like their social and romantic relationships, so a therapist can start to understand the different satisfactions and dissatisfactions that are present in a client's life.

As well as when we start to think about the social withdraw and avoidance behaviours in depression, this can help a therapist to understand potential severity, but also causes. Since if a client has very few social relationships or not a lot of very positive ones then this is information that a therapist would have to factor into any assessment or formulation.

<u>Observations</u>

As great as talking is and the whole assessment interview gives therapists a treasure trove of information, observations are still a vital part of psychology, as well as during the assessment session, observations are important for taking note of particular factors. These factors might remain important throughout the therapy.

A great example of a factor to take note of is a client's presentation. This isn't only about their physical appearance including their dress and level or sometimes sadly lack of self-care, but also their ease in expressing difficulties, like a client's need to be promoted or how spontaneous they are and more.

Also, how a client presents themselves emotionally and their emotional state. Like, is the client angry, anxious, tearful, depressed?

<u>Expectations Of Therapy</u>

This I can fully imagine to be a very weird and tricky area for therapists because everyone has their own myths and ideas about how therapy works. Since even some psychology students I've spoken to in their third and final year of their undergraduate degree still believe in all the myths about therapy. Granted these students don't tend to look at clinical psychology but that only supports my point further.

Myths and misconceptions about therapy are embedded into the very fabric of society so our clients bring these into the therapy room, including the psychological assessment interview.

Therefore, a therapist does ask about the following things during the psychological assessment:

- Why are they seeking help now?
- What are their aims and goals?
- Expectations of therapy?
- Previous experience of therapy and their views about it?

All of these are important to know because whatever the reason they have come forward now might reveal how willing (or not) they are to engage in psychotherapy, and if they have any past experience then you need to know why it "failed" and the mental health condition didn't go away.

Personal History

Understanding a client's personal history is just flat out critical to understanding their mental health condition and difficulties at a core level because some conditions are based in childhood or they're developmental. For example, I'm talking about Adverse Childhood Experiences and how child abuse plays a role in them.

Additionally, family is an important aspect to consider because their family and how functional or not it is could play a role in the condition.

Their education, employment and relationships are also critical to understand. Especially when it comes to depression since people with fewer social relationships tend to be depressed and this could be a manifestation of their social avoidance safety behaviours.

As well as I do want to add that employment could be a factor to consider when it comes to assessing suicide risk. Due to in Suicide Psychology I talk about unemployment is a big predictor of suicide in people.

Finally, understanding a client's medical history

could be useful too as if you know what they have or don't have then this can help to eliminate other causes of these mental health conditions, as required of therapists by the DSM-5.

What Sources Of Information Does a Therapist Use?

When it comes to collecting all the data and information a therapist needs for a psychological assessment, we've spoken a ton about the assessment interview but there are other tools used and some of these will be explored more in two chapters' time.

As a result to get information about a client, a therapist can use the following:

- Self-rating scales
- Direct observation of behaviour
- Symptom rating scales
- Diaries
- Thought records
- Speaking to family members, carers or partners

Overall, at the end of this chapter, you now know a lot about psychological assessments and how critical they are at the start of the therapy, but we've spoken a lot about what is included in an assessment.

Yet, how is an assessment actually done?

HOW IS A PSYCHOLOGICAL ASSESSMENT DONE?

In the last chapter, I explained what a psychological assessment included, why it was important and I briefly spoke about formulation, but now I'm going to talk about how a psychological assessment is actually done so you can understand what tools a therapist uses to gather the information they need.

However, assessments are helpful when it comes to clients and therapists identifying the problem. Then after the problems are identified, the therapist can carry out a more detailed assessment of the mental health difficulties. For example, what happens, who does it happen with, when does it happen and how does the client cope?

Assessments also engage the client so it helps to establish an early therapeutic alliance which is always important.

Overall, these questions are all important for the CBT formulation as they give the therapist an idea about the client's triggers, maintaining factors, feelings, thoughts, body sensations and behaviours.

As well as they help to identify shared goals for the therapy and the answers form an important part of the risk assessment too.

Therefore, the information needed for an assessment is collected using a wide range of tools.

What Is The Assessment Interview?

When it comes to the assessment interview, the conversation and interview between the therapist and client, the therapist is trying to get information about the client's 5Ps. Which as a reminder as:

- Presenting Problems
- Predisposing Factors
- Precipitating Factors
- Perpetuating (Maintaining) Factors
- Protector Factors

As a result, during the interview the therapist is listening out for any key thoughts and behaviours the clients mention are going on. As well as when it comes to identifying a client's problems then the following questions are investigated and asked about:

- What Is The Problem?

This might sound like an easy question but to truly get to the heart of the actual "problem", a therapist would need to ask different questions so the client answers in a more meaningful way than just a fact. For example, if a client says "the problem is my parents are cruel and nasty so I'm depressed," That is brilliant because it's a start, but it doesn't tell you much more than that.

That's why other questions are needed to explore that more, because even before we explore other areas of their life, we still don't know why the parent being cruel and nasty makes them depressed? And also, why does the person believe their cruel and nasty?

- Where does the problem occur?

This is definitely an important question but a therapist does need to be aware of a client's potential memory lapses and generalizations so monitoring and homework could be required.

- What's The Intensity of The Problem?

This question is particularly important when it comes to emotional mental health difficulties or problems of excessive desire, like addiction. As well as this is good to know because this often forms a critical part of the diagnostic criteria and intervention.

- Who's the problem better or worse with?

Now this is a very interesting question because most people never ever think about this idea of certain people might make a mental health condition better or worse, and this tends to be about maintaining and perhaps protective factors too.

Due to if someone always feel *more* depressed when they're at home, then why? This is something that would have to be explored because there are two possible reasons that spring to mind and both have massive implications for the therapy. For example, is being at home a social cause of the depression, or is the home environment somehow maintaining the depression? Such as are the parents and home environment giving the client more love so there is no reason for the client to treat their depression?

That is something that a therapist would have to explore with a client.

- When does the problem happen?

This is particularly important when dealing with anxiety disorders, but it's important for mood disorders as well. Since if the depressive or manic episodes only happen after a specific trigger then again, this has strong implications for the therapeutic intervention.

Psychological Assessments For Depression Symptoms

Additionally, if we focus more on assessments for depression in particular then the following symptoms of a client would also be assessed:

- Negative thoughts
- Feelings of worthlessness or excessive or inappropriate guilt
- Depressed mood
- Loss of interest or pleasure
- Insomnia or hypersomnia
- Changes in behaviour, e.g., social withdrawal; avoidance; reduced activity
- Fatigue or loss of energy
- Psychomotor agitation or retardation
- Change in appetite; significant weight loss or weight gain Diminished ability to think or concentrate or indecisiveness
- Suicidal ideation and suicide risk

How Do Identifying Goals Work In Assessment?

You'll see how this works more later on in the book because there are entire sections dedicated to goals and their importance, but for now, you should know that in psychological assessments the therapist and client work together to identify goals that includes a behaviour. This is important for behavioural activation (there's a chapter dedicated to it later).

Therefore, if a client says their goal of therapy is

to feel better. That is a great goal in the most general of senses but it should include a behaviour, so something more specific and behaviour-oriented is needed.

As well as these goals need to be meaningful, observable and measurable, so if a client doesn't like golf and their goal is to play golf. Then it isn't a very good goal as it isn't meaningful to them in the slightest.

How Are Questionnaires Used In Psychological Assessments And Beyond?

To wrap up this chapter, I'll admit whilst the assessment interview is an important and critical aspect of the assessment, it doesn't give a therapist empirical measures and other important details that help to form an assessment and formulation. As a result, questionnaires and other scales are needed to help the therapist.

These questionnaires are good throughout because at the start of therapy, they help to highlight a client's difficulties and they help to normalize what the client is going through. Since if someone was smart enough to create a scale or questionnaire then there had to be a need for it, so there are a lot of people who filled this need.

Secondly, during therapy, questionnaires are very helpful for the therapist monitoring the progress of the client and to see what the therapy still needs to focus on.

Finally, questionnaires are brilliant at the end of the therapy because they highlight any areas the client still needs to focus on in the future. As well as because CBT equips the client with their own tools and techniques moving forward, they should be able to deal with these areas by themselves.

Yet knowing about these areas are still important so the client can expect them and know how to deal with them in the future.

So now we know how a client is assessed, how can cognitive interventions help a client to change their biased cognitive processes?

CBT FORMULATION

Now this really is one of my favourite topics in clinical psychology because formulation is where mental health needs to go and it is such an important topic within our great profession. As well as if you want to learn a lot more about formulation then please check out Formulation In Psychotherapy.

What Is A Formulation?

To a lot of people "formulation" is a very new concept so for people who don't know, I define it as when a therapist works with a client to tailor a psychotherapy to that particular person. For example, just because a person has depression doesn't mean CBT will always be the same no matter the case since everyone has their own causes and factors that cause a condition to develop.

In addition, a more technical definition is a formulation is a systematic way of relating a person's presenting problem to psychological processes.

Furthermore, regardless of the definition all formulations are based on a theory and they're hypothetical in nature as well as a collaboration between a therapy and a client to create a psychological explanation of the client's presenting problems.

As a result of each client's mental health difficulties are very unique to them so they require an individualized approach. This is definitely something that I think is missed by a lot of students and some lecturers when talking about these psychotherapies. A person can have depression but that doesn't mean CBT is the best option for them. Maybe Acceptance and Commitment Therapy or Mindfulness-Based Cognitive Therapy might be best for that person.

Therefore, a formulation is very helpful in developing a plan for an intervention or therapy. As well as most clinical psychologists work towards explaining the mental health difficulties within theoretical terms but then they try to tailor it to specific clients.

Therefore, all formulations are based on a theoretical understanding of mental health conditions and they can include information about a client's past history. Hence, why we ask about it in the assessment interview.

Also, it's important to know, and I've spoken about this before in different places, but in therapy there is always a power difference and when it comes to formulation, a therapist needs to give the client the power to say no to their formulation or something is wrong.

Just remember this little saying because this has really helped me to understand psychotherapy:

"I'm (the therapist) the expert in the psychological theory but the client is the expert in themselves,"

We don't know the client, their past and their life

so we cannot be experts in them, so this is why a formulation should never be imposed upon a client.

Of course this does depend on a therapist's theoretical orientation because some forms of psychotherapy are a lot more collaborative than others, but it's important that formulations do allow flexibility and each person to understand the client's difficulties.

<u>The 5 Ps Of CBT Formulation</u>

Additionally, the 5Ps of Cognitive Behavioural Therapy like we spoke about earlier are apart of formulation so formulations look at the following areas in particular:

- Presenting issues. These are statements about the client's presenting problems in terms of their thoughts, behaviours and emotions.
- Precipitating factors. These are external and internal factors that triggered the current presenting issues.
- Perpetuating factors: These are the internal and external factors that maintain the current problems.
- Predisposing factors. These are external and internal factors that increase the person's vulnerability to their current problems.
- Protective factors. These are critical because they involve a person's resilience and strengths that help maintain emotional health.

As a result of these 5Ps, therapists can develop a suggested explanation of how their condition and difficulties develop and are maintained in collaboration with the client. This tends to be done using diagrams (like the Hot Cross Bun Formulation)

that outlines:
- The formulation's content
- The client's specific triggers
- Their cognitive processes and thoughts
- The onset factors such as vulnerability and early experiences.
- Specific triggers
- Behaviours
- Emotions how these all interact

And it's this showing of how these factors interact that can be really powerful to the client, because let's face it psychology can be very abstract at times and unless you have experience in it, it's hard to wrap your head around all these different factors.

That's why formulation tools and diagrams are so valuable and to be honest, fun to do with clients since they are so visual. They really help clients to understand what's going on. That's why the Hot Cross Bun formulation is a good one to use.

COGNITIVE INTERVENTIONS FOR DEPRESSION

Now I seriously love this next chapter because it really shows how brilliant, creative and potentially fun CBT can actually be for therapists and clients. Due to there are so many different cognitive interventions that therapists can use to work with clients to challenge and change their negative automatic thoughts and other biased cognitive processes.

As a result, in this chapter, we're going to explore some really interesting cognitive interventions and then some of these will be explored in greater depth in the following chapters.

For example, we have an entire chapter dedicated to behavioural activation, involving goal setting and psychoeducation which helps us to share information with the client and it helps to normalize what they're going through. That's a critical component of CBT.

In addition, skills training in CBT is another great tool to use and intervention, but my personal favourite are behavioural experiments and there's a very passionate chapter involving them later on. Yet for now, just know that behavioural experiments are a form of behavioural activation that aim to make a client look at and reappraise their mental images and thoughts about themselves, others and the world, so all these cognitive interventions are connected to the client's presenting problems.

Moreover, all cognitive interventions should be based on a shared formulation because the client must understand the reasoning behind the cognitive work. Especially since as current or future therapists, we are asking them to explore the most depressing, shameful and frightening aspects of themselves. That isn't easy for anyone.

As well as as mentioned earlier therapists typically start with a client's Negative Automatic Thoughts before moving on to deeper levels of cognition, leaving core beliefs until later in therapy and then only if necessary.

How Is Goal Setting used In CBT?

Whilst we talk more about goal setting in CBT in the Behavioural Activation chapter, it's important to know now that goal setting helps to decide and maintain the focus of the therapy and the formulation. Since the therapist knows what to include in the therapy or formulation to help the client get to where they want to go.

Furthermore, goal setting is important because it helps to reinforce to the client that this is a collaborative therapy and the client does have a valid say in what happens. As well as this helps to increase client engagement because their working towards the same goals that were developed together and goal setting makes the therapy relevant to the client. So they're even more motivated to engage in it.

In addition, goal setting flat out implies to the

client that there is a strong possibility of change and this helps to give them hope and reduce their feelings of helplessness. Due to surely the therapist wouldn't want us to work towards a goal if there was no hope of me getting "better"?

As well as it raises the idea of an end to treatment, which always excites clients.

Finally for this section, goal setting helps clients to feel that their "problems" or mental health difficulties are more manageable when they're broken down into more specific parts.

Goal setting is an extremely powerful tool to use early on in a course of therapy.

What's The Typical Structure Of A CBT Session?

Something that is rarely discussed in learning about CBT is how an actual session works, because students learn about how CBT works over the course of treatment and the different tools and techniques work, but how about the sessions themselves?

Therefore, a typical session works in the following way. For example, firstly a client updates the therapist with how they are and how they feel they're processing amongst other things for 5 minutes.

Secondly, the therapist and client spend 5 minutes agreeing the agenda for this session.

Thirdly, the therapist and client review the homework and understand it. Then they work their way through the agenda for the session all before spending at least ten minutes agreeing on this week's homework task.

Then they conclude the session in the last five minutes by reflecting on the session and summarizing what they've done and learnt.

What Are Thought Records?

Personally, I think thought records are brilliant because this is one type of cognitive intervention that makes a person focus on their thoughts, and this is so much easier for clients now that everyone has a smartphone. As well as a thought record is quite literally a person recording their thoughts and certain details about it.

These records used to be done using pen and paper but the problem with that is a person is very unlikely to do it in public because they don't want to alert people around them, they're having to record their thoughts and come on, if a person is depressed because their biased cognitive processes are telling them everything they do is pointless because they're a failure, they seriously aren't going to get a pen and paper out.

And then it could be argued that them not being able to get a pen and paper is just another sign that they're useless and their biased cognitive processes will only get confirmed (to some extent).

Thankfully this is less of a problem now with thought records being largely done on people's phones and phones are so common now we don't really bat an eyelid if we see someone typing on their phone.

In addition, here are the key stages of the cognitive restructuring process that happens when a person is using a Thought Record Identification of the event.

- They connect to the feeling the thought triggered.
- They identify the Negative Automatic Thought or Image and explore its meaning. This is known as the identification of the "hot thought"
- They find evidence for the "hot thought"
- Evidence against the "hot thought"
- Write a balanced statement
- Re-evaluate their feelings

And as you can imagine the vast majority of the time, the person finds there is more evidence against the Negative Automatic Thoughts or Image then there is supporting it.

A quick teaching-only example for depression would be if someone believes that they're useless at everything and this thought occurred when they got a 2:1 mark on an essay. They would record the thought and how depressed it makes them. Then they might realise that yes, they wanted the First-class mark and they didn't get it (evidence for it).

However, they'll then realise that a 2:1 is still a good mark and the comments were very positive (evidence against the thought) so they conclude the thought wasn't correct and they shouldn't feel scared and anxious.

Afterwards, the therapist and client discuss these thoughts in therapy using the client's recent examples and these Thought Records can be kept in a Thought Diary. With it being most likely to be accurate if the records were made as soon as possible.

Therefore, thought records help clients tune into their thoughts, so they understand when and in what situations their Negative Automatic Thoughts are likely to occur.

Furthermore, people are often confused by their feelings and thoughts because feelings can often be expressed in one word (like an emotion) so people find it easier to notice the feeling first and then by exploring the feelings and elaborating on them the thoughts often emerge.

As well as it's important for clients to try and make the thoughts as specific as possible in their records. For example, instead of saying "I'm useless", it's best to say something like "I'm useless at maths".

Thoughts Aren't Facts

This is essentially the point of the cognitive interventions, because the therapist is always trying to challenge the client's biased cognitive processes and thought records are a great way to show them that their thoughts are not fact.

Moreover, this is supported by the Grandfather of CBT himself (that's what I jokingly call him anyway), since Beck describes cognitions as "either a thought or a visual image that you may not be very aware of unless you focus your attention on it'".

As a result, for a client to be able to identify a though that might not be a fact, this does require some distance from it and this is why it's important the client provides themselves with this space where alternatives can start to be considered.

Especially as therapists need to help guard clients against seeing their thoughts as "wrong" or "irrational" as this may feed in to negative beliefs. For example, if a client believes "they're stupid" or "they're useless at everything", the last thing you want is for them to use their own biased cognitive processes to confirm the exact same processes we're working on.

Furthermore, it's good to acknowledge that just because a client has a belief that isn't helpful now, it doesn't mean that was always the case. A biased belief might have been helpful once and sometimes a cognition might only be unhelpful if it's held with too much conviction.

Overall, cognitive interventions are all about pulling away the layers from a situation and giving the client a helicopter view of their cognitive processes and this helps to make their thinking broader, more balanced as well as more flexible.

How Are new Perspectives Developed?

So we have a client recording their thoughts and doing other cognitive interventions, good for us, so what now?

After a client has explored their thoughts, they need to explore the alternatives to their beliefs and this is typically started off with a therapist asking these "simple" questions:

- Can you think of other possibilities?
- Other explanations?
- What doesn't fit with your first belief conclusion?
- Have you been in similar situations and not thought or felt like this?
- Are there things you may be overlooking when you are distressed?

- If someone you cared about had this thought what would you say to them?
- When you are away from this situation, what do you think?

As you can imagine, these questions aren't easy for anyone and even more so for depressed people, so it might take a therapist a little while to get through all these questions with a client, but once they do they can do "Socratic Questioning".

In other words, what's the evidence for this alternative explanation?

The interesting thing about this sort of evidence searching is that the client actually already has the knowledge to answer. Since these alternative explanations do draw the client's attention to the information which is relevant to what's being discussed but this information to the Socratic question just might be outside of their current focus.

Generally as new perspectives are developed, this starts in the concrete realm so the things that there is real physical evidence for, and then it slowly moves towards the more abstract side of things, and this enables the client to re-evaluate their previous conclusion and beliefs.

Problem: What if The Belief Is True?

Now this is a fascinating section to wrap up this chapter with because what does a therapist do if their client's thoughts are actually accurate. For example, what if they're useless at driving?

What's happening here is one of three options. Firstly, their thought is accurate but it's the conclusion that the client draws from it that's flawed and distorted. Meaning that to develop a new perspective, it's the validity of the conclusion that needs to be evaluated, not the actual thought.

For instance, if we go back to the driving example, a client might be useless at driving at this moment in time so they believe they'll always be useless (I know the feeling) they're useless at everything because of their bad driving. Neither one of them is true.

Secondly, the thought could be validated but it could be unhelpful and the client could overvalue its importance. Therefore, it would be important to evaluate its helpfulness and alternative perspectives.

Such as when it comes to driving, yes a client might be useless at driving, but is it that important? If they live in a city with great public transport and they don't intend to leave, then it isn't that important? That's something a therapist might be able to help them understand.

Finally, a therapist could use another technique to help solve this problem, like problem-solving if developing a new perspective isn't working.

And that's something I love about psychology and therapy, there is no magic bullet that works with every client and that's what makes our profession so interesting, fun and exciting because it's true. Every day is different.

BEHAVIOURAL EXPERIMENTS

This chapter covers another type of cognitive intervention that I absolutely love because Behavioural Experiments are so cool, amazing and just flat out brilliant. I love learning about them and if you ever find a good video of these being done properly or you get to use them or see them in real life, you'll realise how amazing they are too.

However, for the sake of clarity, a behavioural experiment are:

"Planned experiential activities, based on experimentation or observation, which are undertaken by clients in or between sessions" (Bennett-Levy, J., Butler, G. Fennell, M., Hackmann, A., Mueller, M. & Westbrook, D., 2004).

As well as these are very powerful to combating safety behaviours and their design is directly generated from cognitive formulations of presenting problems. In other words, behavioural experiments are done to counteract the client's presenting problems as seen in a hot-cross-bun formulation, for example.

Why Use Behavioural Experiments?

Personally, I would say why wouldn't you use them, but as great as thought records are because they allow the client to become more aware of their thinking and patterns of behaviour, and even come up with their own alternatives to these thoughts and behaviours. The person can still not be fully convinced that the alternatives are true.

As a result, behavioural experiments can:

- Test a client's unhelpful existing beliefs.
- Test out their new and more helpful beliefs
- Collect information to help develop the formulation further
- They enable experiential learning. Basically learning by doing.
- Allow clients to test out theory A versus Theory B

One of the ways and something that is very common in CBT is that a client will argue forever that they know what you're saying and the alternatives are true at a logical and fact level and they "feel it in my heart" and they "know it in their head" but they still refuse to believe it.

That's why behavioural experiments are very powerful ways to get them to see what happens when they drop their safety behaviours.

Of course, I'm not saying that behavioural experiments are easy for both the therapist and the client. Since the therapist needs to design behavioural experiments so, so carefully because if one of these experiments goes wrong then you have basically just confirmed outright a person's biased cognitive errors and beliefs. That isn't what you want.

Additionally, these can be difficult for the client because your therapist is basically making you confront something you absolutely hate.

However, I know this doesn't directly apply to depression but if you ever see get a chance to see these experiments in practice as a student then definitely watch them. Since the one I watched was with an anxious woman who believed she would have sweat pouring off her, she would be violently shaking like an earthquake and she would be tomato red when she had to talk to a stranger so the therapist filmed an interaction and it turned out the woman was completely wrong.

She wasn't bright tomato red, she wasn't shaking (you really couldn't tell she was shaking at all) and no visual sweat was coming off her. This made the woman very surprised and happy and the therapist got the woman to do the experiment twice, once with safety behaviours and one without.

And you know what happened?

The woman admitted she looked so much more personable, likeable and human when she did the experiment without her safety behaviours.

It was a very powerful and fascinating thing to watch and enjoy.

On the whole, the purpose of behavioural experiments is to get new information so the client can test the validity of their existing beliefs and cognitions. This includes them testing the content of these beliefs and cognitions and seeing the effect of their maladaptive processes. As well as behavioural experiments allow clients to create and test new, more adaptive beliefs and cognitions.

Finally, if we apply this information to depression (the entire purpose of the book) then these experiments allow people to get new information to test the validity of alternative explanations of depression through behavioural activation and associated symptoms.

BEHAVIOURAL ACTIVATION AND HOW IS IT DONE?

Moving onto our next chapter, I have to admit that this is a brilliant one because whenever a person learns about CBT and is given the basic definition, there are two concepts that always come up. Cognitive restructuring and behavioural activation.

Now whilst cognitive restructuring is the main component and a lot of research has said this is the most important one out of the two, we're already spoken about it and to be honest, I love the concept of behavioural activation. Since it is basically us getting someone to perform the behaviour we want them to do (there's a hell of a lot more to it than that), and as a sci-fi writer, I love the idea of controlling someone.

How Depression Causes Avoidance And Withdrawal Behaviour?

Anyway, away from the silly stuff, behavioural activation is flat out critical in CBT because the "problem" with depression, and all mental health conditions, is that there are maintaining factors for low mood that lead to a reduction in activity and a depressed person engages in social withdrawal and avoidance.

In other words, a low mood leads to a behavioural reduction in activity leading to a loss of achievement, enjoyment and social isolation leading to a low mood.

In addition, the social withdrawal a depressed person engages in includes them not answering the phone (some textbooks say telephone but seriously, who uses a landline these days?) and they avoid their friends.

However, depressed people also take part in non-social avoidance behaviour. For example, they don't take on challenging tasks (because in their mind, what's the point I'm useless and worthless anyway?), they sit around the house and spend excessive time in bed. All in an effort to avoid people and to withdraw from their lives.

In addition, depression causes people to engage in cognitive avoidance as well that's different from the other two. Since depressed people don't think about relationship problems (so they aren't being fixed either), they don't make decisions about the future, taking opportunities, being serious about their education or work and they're driven to avoidance by distraction as well.

Due to depressed people show more avoidance behaviours by watching television, gambling, playing computer games, excessive exercise (interesting considering some depressed people have a lack of energy and exercise is good for your mental health) and comfort eating. As well as drug and alcohol abuse.

Overall, as you can see depression causes people

to engage in a wide range of negative and rather self-destructive avoidance and withdrawal behaviours, so in order to effectively treat depression, therapists need to change all of this.

This is why behavioural activation has amazing potential.

What Is Behavioural Activation?

We now know why behavioural activation is so important, and behavioural activation focuses on pleasurable activities that are consistent with the way a client wants to live. Therefore, a therapist and a client tackle a list of tasks in a responsible way using 6 to 12 weekly sessions and this involves working towards specific goals from week to week.

And whilst I talk a lot more about this "Goal-Orient Approach" and its importance in *Clinical Psychology Reflections Volume 4*, I want to stress that giving or helping a client to realise a goal is immensely powerful. Due to you're giving them the ability to work towards physical, seeable and something they can see will make a big impact on their life instead of something as meaningless to them as decreasing their depression scores on a random test that they don't care about.

As a result, that is why when it comes to behavioural activation, therapists help the client to identify activities that are uniquely important to the client by typically asking:

- What matters most to you?
- What kind of life do you want to build for yourself?

And just a quick little thought exercise for yourself, what would you actually say to that therapist? Personally, if I was too depressed to write, podcast and go out with my friends and family then that would honestly be my priority.

I seriously couldn't imagine not writing and podcasting, and if you've listened to the podcast then you know my passion comes through.

But what would your response be?

Furthermore, after those questions, the therapist and client work together to come up with specific activities that really matter to them and are based on a client's values and desires. Consequently, it's always important to make sure the client's goals are manageable and specific.

Then the activities are listed easiest to hardest and it's important to come up with a range of activities from different aspects of the client's life. For example, study, work, relationships, family, personal care as well as friendships. Bearing in mind the client needs to be mindful of avoidance behaviours and they need to reward their progress.

For instance, an example could be if the client was once a major gardener that was an important and valued and loved member of their local gardening club. Yet since their depression they hadn't been to one of the weekly meetings in over two years.

Then an activity might be just to go to one single meeting for at least half an hour. They might not have to talk to anyone, they can just go and be back in the environment again (but chances are once they are in the environment, they will see old friends and might slowly start engaging in conversation again).

That's one example of how we might go about helping a client to reverse the negative impacts of their withdrawal and avoidance behaviour.

<u>What is Activity Scheduling And Behavioural</u>

Activation?

Moving onto some of the literature for behavioural activation, the idea of activity scheduling is from Veale (2008) based on the research by Jacobson et al. (1996). When the researchers randomised 150 people with depression to three groups:

- Activity Scheduling
- Activity Scheduling AND cognitive challenges to automatic thoughts (basically half CBT)
- Activity scheduling AND cognitive challenges to automatic thoughts, core beliefs and assumptions. Basically full CBT.

Overall, Jacobson et al. (1996) found no statistically or clinically significant differences between the groups and they concluded that the cognitive component was redundant.

HOWEVER, I have to admit that recently this has really been up for debate because I've found a lot of research that concludes that cognitive restructuring is the most important aspect of CBT with the meta-analysis of Ciharova et al. (2021) being a great example.

Therefore, I would say whilst the jury is still out on what's most important in CBT, the majority of modern research I have seen says cognitive restructuring is the most important aspect. But behavioural activation is still a critical aspect.

And to be honest, I understand it's important to know what components work the best, but as a therapist you should still never get rid of a tool in your arsenal because for certain clients behavioural activation might be the critical technique you need to employ that changes everything for a client.

Just a thought.

What Are The Challenges Of Behavioural Activation?

Of course, nothing ever goes perfectly in any kind of therapy and that is partly what makes our current or future jobs so interesting, but when it comes to behavioural activation there are five main problems that can arise.

Firstly, the activities the client picks for themselves just aren't that pleasurable to them. This is a problem not only because they lack motivation to do it but also it sadly makes them less likely to do it and they continue their withdrawal and avoidance behaviours.

Secondly, either the therapist or client has excessive standards. I would say this is possibly more of a client "problem" because you will always get clients that think therapy is an "instant" fix so they should be able to do whatever they want quickly. But it doesn't work like that, and this can make them disheartened which is always a problem.

Thirdly (and sort of fourthly) a client tries to do too much too soon or too little. The problem with doing too much too soon is that a "failure" is likely to lead to the client doubting the therapy, becoming emotionally hurt or even worse, having their biased cognitive beliefs confirmed. Either way this negatively impacts the therapy. As well as the problem with doing too little is that there's a very real risk that the client might feel like they're not making progress, and what's the point of therapy if I'm not making progress?

Not exactly the sort of question you want as a therapist.

Finally, vague planning can be very dangerous

and this is why, just like for behavioural experiments, these behavioural activation tasks are normally planned greatly. Since planning these tasks properly helps to minimise the chance of something going wrong and it certainly makes sure there is less chance of a Negative Automatic Thought being confirmed.

For example, if someone's NAT or core belief was "the world hates me" and your client goes to a garden club, gets into an argument and they storm out of there. That is likely to confirm their belief about the world hating them.

And bang goes a lot of your therapy work, so planning is critical.

Thankfully, behavioural activation is a powerful therapy tool for CBT therapists to use and it can really help clients reverse the avoidance and withdrawal behaviours that maintain their depression, so their psychological distress can decrease and they can improve their lives.

WHEN DOES PSYCHOTHERAPY END?

This next chapter helps to introduce you to the concept of ending psychotherapy before we wrap up the book and look at endings in CBT in particular.

This was an episode of The Psychology World Podcast and this was a truly fascinating one so I hope you enjoy it.

(And if you want to learn more from The Psychology World Podcast, you can find it on all major podcast apps and YouTube.)

<u>When Does Psychotherapy End?</u>

Whilst I've spoken about the end of psychotherapy before and its importance in one of my Clinical Psychology Reflections books, I wanted to talk about it again from a different angle because endings are important in therapy. So in today's podcast episode we explore why clients and us as current or future therapists know that when it's time to end psychotherapy for a client. This is a great episode for anyone interested in clinical psychology.

What I Am Shaking My Hands Off In This Episode?

Now I want to fully admit this, and especially after my recent lectures, that I was forgetting on purpose a hell of a lot of real things that goes on in the clinical psychology workplace. So please, don't think I'm stupid and naïve because of this podcast topic and to be honest, very little of this episode applies if you work or want to work in the public sector. Since in the public sector and the NHS in the UK, you give your client 6 sessions maybe 8 if you beg your boss and that's it.

It doesn't matter if those sessions work or are actually at the end of the therapy for the client. You have six sessions and that's it.

Therefore, please know that I'm talking about in an ideal world this is how you know you're at the end of the therapy. Or this works if you're in the private sector, but I still believe it's important to learn about so all of us are at least aware of these signs.

How Psychotherapy Works?

Whilst I know a lot of the podcast audience are psychology students and professionals I still want to recap this topic briefly in case there's anyone who isn't too familiar with what exactly psychotherapy is. Therefore, psychotherapy is a uniquely collaborative environment centred around learning since the psychotherapist teaches and works with the client to give them new skills, concepts and knowledge that could help the client to navigate their lives a little easier (American Psychological Association, 2012). For example, a client might get help to improve their emotional awareness, finding a purpose, improving their problem solving or improving their interpersonal relationships.

In addition, therapists use different approaches and types of psychotherapy depending on the demands of the client (or in the public sector you'll get what you're given). For instance, psychodynamic therapy is where you explore your underlying wishes, fears and fantasies as well as your unconscious thoughts (Brown et al., 2014). This form of therapy is effective at improving and addressing people's relationships. Whereas Cognitive Behavioural Therapy investigates a person's maladaptive thought processes and dysfunctional behaviours. Making it great to treat anxiety, depression and other mental health conditions.

Additionally, whilst different therapies target different aspects of a mental health condition, they all have three things in common or at least share similar aspects. They all involve a relationship between a client and a therapist, they involve the implementation of goals and health promoting actions as well as they involve setting both expectations and goals in each therapy session (Wampold, 2014).

How Do We Know If It's Beneficial To End Therapy?

Again, unless you're in the public sector, deciding

to end therapy is a decision that should always be made carefully by both the therapist and the client. Ending it too soon is problematic because the client's difficulties might return quickly and the client will not benefit from the therapy if it isn't completed. Equally, there's no point continuing with the therapy if there's no need for it.

It is always best to decide if the time is right to end therapy with a conversation between the psychologist and client, and they need to both agree this is the right time. This is a collaborative process after all.

As a result, now we're going to cover three questions that might help you as the therapist or client to decide if the time is right.

<u>Is The Treatment Relationship Going Awry?</u>

This is the first question I wanted to ask because at the end of the day, a therapeutic relationship is still a relationship. All relationships can go wrong at times and they can form, be maintained and break down. The therapeutic relationship is not immune to this breakdown.

Interestingly enough, if this conflict does activate then this is normally the start of a "real" therapeutic relationship and the therapy itself. Since if the therapist struck a nerve then this is an area that is often reflected in the client's real world relationships and this conflict spreads to other contexts.

Therefore, speaking and working through this conflict is important and of course, this requires a lot of trust from the client.

However, what you don't want as a therapist, is for this conflict to be because of a lack of skills on your end. Such as, a therapist needs to maintain and hold emotional boundaries with the client so this doesn't lead to confusion about who's difficulties are being assessed and solved. If this is the problem and a client can talk to their therapist about this, and if the conflict still isn't being resolved. Then it might be an idea for the client to find a therapist who has the skills they require.

Is The Client Running Away?

When therapy actually starts properly, it is natural for clients to get scared and as psychology students and professionals, we have to acknowledge that fact. As well as it's important to bear in mind that a client's past behaviour can predict their future behaviour because if a client has ghosted or left people in their own life, then they want to do the same to you as their therapist.

Clearly if a client does do this then these behaviours are maladaptive and avoidance-focused. As well as the client might do this because the therapeutic relationship feeds into their fears of abandonment and continue their cycle of avoidance, because the therapy will end at some point and that's scary. But the client needs to ask themselves, *what exactly are they running away from?*

And hopefully, they can be convinced (hopefully without any external involvement) that it's important to stick around so they can find out what they're running away from.

Is The Client Improving?

Typically, this final question is asked in such a biomedical model way that I hate it, but it is important. As a result of the client came to us because they had a mental health condition severe enough to get a diagnosis, so this was causing them disruption in their daily lives.

Therefore, when they leave the therapy room (in an ideal world) they would be better, they would know how to live with their condition because you cannot get rid of mental health conditions and they would be able to live a clinically "normal" life.

However, some clients start to question therapy when lives get tough, when they make a little bit of process but not as much as they like, or when they believe they haven't made any progress at all. When this happens they should of course talk to their therapist and there should be a conversation as to why this might be the case and it is possible that the client is experiencing psychological resistance. Possibly leading to avoiding emotions and/ or rejecting the change that therapy brings.

If this is happening then it's good for clients and therapists to know that this could be a part of a larger emotional as well as cognitive process people call ambivalence. This happens for a range of reasons but being able to recognise when ambivalence is happening and acknowledge it is important. As this is the first step for the client overcoming the resistance with the help of their therapist.

Conclusion

I know I ignored a lot of real-world public sector things in this podcast episode, and that is an important detail for the UK audience at the very least, but this is what should happen in an ideal world. As well as I'm sure that the members of the audience working in the private sector can tell us stories about clients ending the therapy when they really shouldn't have.

This is sadly nothing new.

However, this is important for us to remember as future or current psychologists, because if we work with clients then there will be a point in our careers when we have to ask this question. And we will have to gently tell the client that they really shouldn't be ending the therapy because there is still work to be done. Maybe those three questions will help you and your client come to a shared realisation or maybe this episode was just good background knowledge for a rainy day.

I don't know but what I do know is that at the end of the day, we can only go so far and if a client truly wants to end therapy because they aren't ready for the change. Then there is nothing we can do to help them until they're ready.

ENDING SESSIONS AND THERAPY IN CBT

I first came across the idea of ending therapy a few years ago and I honestly found it fascinating, because I naturally presumed like everyone else in the lecture that endings weren't that important in therapy. Since by the time the therapy was done, it was just done, the client had all the tools and techniques they needed to live a functional happy life and it was over.

But endings are arguably one of the most important aspects of therapy because if an ending is wrong then it can mess up the entire therapy process, and that is just fascinating.

Endings in both the therapy overall and the therapy session is just critical. That's why I've dedicated two chapters to it.

<u>What Happens At The End of A Therapy Session?</u>

Earlier in the book we spoke about what happens in a therapy session overall, so now let's zoom in and see what exactly happens at the end of a therapy session.

Firstly, a therapist asks the client to summarise what they've understood today and the therapist summarises it too, so that way the therapist knows what has and hasn't been understood, and it's important to know if everything had both parties wanted to address on the agenda has or hasn't been addressed.

Therefore, the following questions might be asked to help make sure the client has understood everything and learnt from the session:

- "Perhaps you could tell me what you have understood from today's session?"
- "Could you summarise what you will remember of today's main points"
- "What will you take away from today's session?"

Secondly, the homework is set for the next week and they address any barriers to adherence. For example, a set of homework might be, to count how many times they think of negative thoughts in the next week. It's an example from an earlier session but it is designed to help the client recognise their thoughts and this is done through thought records.

In addition, when it comes to setting the homework, the decision on what task should be set must be done in a collaborative way with the therapist explaining the possible tasks in detail so the client knows what's expected and how it should help. For example, it would help with motivation, their understanding of CBT and then in later sessions in

CBT, the client gets to generate their own homework tasks. As well as a practical demonstration of the homework task might be done to show the client what needs to be done.

Furthermore, a client and therapist would talk about any obstacles to carrying out the task and how the client could overcome them. Then in the next session, the therapist sees what the client actually did and learnt from it.

Finally, at the end of a therapy session, the therapist would get the client to feedback on the session and their therapeutic relationship. For instance, a therapist might say:

"It would be helpful if you can give me some feedback about how today's session has gone. Perhaps give me one or two things that you liked about today and one or two things that you felt uncomfortable about, either about something we did, something I said or how I was with you?"

Overall, the reason why this is important is because in clinical psychology, there is the reflective-practitioner model that requires psychologists to be constantly evolving, learning and wanting to become better. And I suppose this works both on the career level so each client teaches you something you can use going forward, but this also happens on the individual-client-level since some things work with some clients, other things don't.

So this is why you need to ask what works and what is helpful for a particular client so you can use that information going forward.

Moreover, towards the end of the therapy, the therapist is increasingly preparing the client to become their own therapist so they can continue to make sure they're okay and don't relapse after the therapy finishes.

How Ending The Therapy Works?

Now this is a critical part of the overall course of treatment because if there is a jerking ending or an unsatisfying end then this can be just as damaging as no therapy at all. For example, one of my lecturers told us how her client had had so many therapists and they just ended up leaving him that it confirmed his cognitive processes about how everyone leaves him in the end.

That isn't what an ending is meant to look like in CBT, so that's why we need to focus on it now. There's no point doing therapy if the ending is only going to undo all the hard work of the client and therapist.

Therefore, the ending of therapy should be like the beginning in terms of it being structured and collaborative. As well as when a therapist does end of a piece with a client they would revisit the goals they set with the client set at the beginning.

To make sure that they've gotten everything they've set out to achieve, and it's nice that you can go to the client, something along the lines of "Look, a few months ago you told me these were all impossible to achieve and now look at you,"

And this links into making the client realise how much *they're* done and why *they're* amazing.

And that's the magic thing about CBT, it is a therapy where the client is always centre-stage because the therapist might give them great tools, but at the end of the day, it is the client that put in the work and made the change all possible.

Sometimes it only takes the skilled hand of a

therapist to make them realise just how incredible they actually are.

CONCLUSION

At this moment in time as I write this book, I've only written *CBT For Anxiety* and this book and to it wrap up, I want to say that if you haven't already read the other CBT books in the series then definitely do that. Since as a writer, each book requires me to learn more and more about the fascinating different aspects of CBT.

Due to if you read the CBT For Anxiety book then you see that we focused a little more on the conditions and a little more on the theory behind CBT. Yet in this book, there's more focus on the CBT itself which makes both books fascinating to read and learn about.

Therefore, as a little "love letter" to CBT, I know a lot of people have issues with CBT, and I completely get that because at times it does seem that the entire psychotherapy world revolves around CBT. But there are reasons for that, CBT is the most-evidenced approach we have to therapy, it works and interestingly enough it is so adaptable.

CBT has given rise to second and third wave therapies and I cannot see that stopping any time soon.

And as a future psychologist that makes me so excited about the future of our great profession.

Therefore, please keep learning, continue to be passionate about psychology and have fun because our profession is so rewarding that it is honestly one of the best jobs ever as a lot of people tell me.

So let's be part of that.

EVALUATE CBT FOR MAJOR DEPRESSION DISORDER

Major Depression Disorder (MDD) is a mood disorder (Davey et al., 2015) characterised by the DSM-5 as loss of interest and pleasure in activities the client used to enjoy, depressed mood, fatigue, feeling worthless or excessive guilt amongst other psychological symptoms (APA, 2013). Leading to an increased risk of suicide (Harrington, 2001), poor school performance and social functioning (Smit et al., 2003) and problematic substance use (Chassin et al., 2001) resulting in researchers arguing MDD has a high burden on society (Thapar et al., 2012). The prevalence of MDD varies according to country, age and occupation but MDD in children has a prevalence of 2.8% rising to 5.6% in adolescence (Jane Costello et al., 2006) and an average lifetime prevalence of 12% (Bains and Abdijadid, 2022). Therefore, this essay will critically evaluate the effectiveness of Cognitive Behavioural Therapy (CBT) by briefly outlining treatments for MDD before examining the strengths and limitations of CBT and the associated literature before concluding the effectiveness of CBT in treating MDD.

A multitude of psychological and pharmacological interventions have been developed to treat MDD. For example, Selective Serotonin Reuptake Inhibitors (SSRIs) are a popular biological intervention underpinning anti-depressants (Moncrieff et al., 2022). SSRIs are based on the theory MDD is caused by chemical imbalances in the brain (Moncrieff et al., 2022) based on a study finding a link between lowered serotonin and depression in the 1960s (Coppen, 1967) and more contemporary research supports this view to an extent with Caspi et al. (2003) providing evidence of short alleles, versions, of the 5-HTT gene were more likely to have depression than other participants with different alleles. This research was widely publicised in the 1990s with the rise of SSRI antidepressants (APA, 2021; GlaxoSmithKline, 2009; Lilly, 2006). SSRIs are designed to increase serotonin levels in the brain to restore the imbalance and decrease depressive symptoms (Moncrieff et al., 2022). However, modern academic research does not support this serotonin theory with many academics questioning its validity and empirical basis (Healy, 2015; Moncrieff et al., 2022; Pies, 2011) and yet the theory remains influential because leading textbooks still support it (Geddes and Andreasen, 2020; Hodo, 2006; Sadock et al., 2017), a plethora of research continues to be based on it (Amidfar et al., 2018; Hahn et al., 2014; Yohn et al., 2017) and leading researchers endorse the theory (Albert et al., 2012; Cowen and Browning, 2015; Harmer et al., 2017; Yohn et al., 2017). Overall, whilst the empirical evidence for SSRI antidepressants is lacking, this will continue to be a treatment for MDD for the foreseeable future. Especially as 80% of the general public believe in the chemical imbalance theory (Pescosolido et al., 2010; Pikington et al., 2013).

Alternatively, MDD can be effectively treated with Mindfulness-Based Cognitive Therapy (MBCT) (Kuyken et al., 2008; Ma and Teasdale, 2004; Teasdale et al., 2000) designed by Segal et al. (2002) based on the cognitive vulnerability model (Segal et al., 2013) to prevent recurrence and relapse in MDD. This "third wave" CB therapy focuses on developing new ways of being and relating to the client's thoughts and feelings by combining cognitive-behavioural therapy with mindfulness-based stress reduction strategies in an 8-week program (Sipe and Eisendrath, 2012) and simple yoga and meditation (van der Velden et al., 2015). Whilst placing little emphasis on challenging or offering alternative cognitions of the client (Sipe and Eisendrath, 2012). MBCT is thought to be effective because it improves meta-cognitive awareness (van der Velden et al., 2015) referring to a client's ability to observe thoughts and feelings as temporary and automatic events that are not true descriptions of reality or facts (Teasdale et al., 2002). This links with Beck et al. (1985)'s work on the Cognitive Triad and the associated negative automatic thoughts causing MDD. Also MBCT aids in specificity of life goals and goal attainment, a factor identified as a feature of suicidality and depression (van der Velden et al., 2015), and increases the risk of relapse in MDD (Crane et al., 2012). After clients went through MBCT, they reported having more life goals than waitlist controls (van der Velden et al., 2015) suggesting MBCT is useful in treating MDD by targeting a plethora of causes like making a person aware of their negative automatic thoughts are passing and helping them develop more life-goals (van der Velden et al., 2015).

Nevertheless, Cognitive Behavioural Therapy is a highly effective psychotherapy for MDD (Lepping et al., 2017; Lopez-Lopez et al., 2019; NICE, 2018; Whiston et al., 2019) this essay will critically review in the rest of this paper. CBT is recommended as a gold standard treatment for MDD by the NICE guidelines (2022) involving a directive, time-limited, structured approach emphasising a collaborative therapeutic relationship between the psychotherapist and client (Fenn and Byrne, 2013) assuming maladaptive behaviours are learnt so they can be unlearned (Apolinário-Hagen et al., 2020). Therefore, therapist and client work to understand the client's experiences and how to overcome overwhelming problems by breaking them down into smaller components (Davey et al., 2015). Clients learn how to identify unhelpful and unrealistic thinking processes and patterns maintaining their MDD (Davey et al., 2015) as well, so they can use the techniques they are taught in therapy to challenge these negative thoughts and change their habits in everyday life (Davey et al., 2015). Ultimately, CBT works by helping a client become more aware of the interrelationships between their thoughts, feelings and behaviours (Davey et al., 2015), including their negative cognitive styles, a cause of MDD identified by Alloy et al. (1999), and the Cognitive Triad as identified by Beck et al. (1985).

CBT has a plethora of advantages in MDD treatment. For example, CBT is a highly effective psychotherapy for MDD according to a multitude of studies and meta-analyses. One such meta-analysis is Whiston et al. (2019) who reviewed 138 studies looking at the effectiveness of CBT and Interpersonal psychotherapy for treating MDD, finding CBT alone was superior to any form of IPT treatment and Treatment-As-Usual (TAU) groups and CBT effectively reduced depressive symptoms. Therefore, this study demonstrates not only is CBT an effective treatment, it is a more effective treatment compared to other psychotherapies. Also, unlike pharmacology interventions causing side effects (Cascade et al., 2009; Kelly et al., 2022; Wang et al., 2018), this review failed to find any empirical evidence for negative side effects in CBT for MDD. The closest this review found in the CBT literature was Knouse et al. (2018) discussing side effects in ADHD clients but this article noted how none of these "side effects" could be empirically linked to CBT. Overall, CBT is more effective and has few side effects than other interventions (Whiston et al., 2019; CITE).

Further, Lopez-Lopez et al. (2019) found similar results but their meta-analyses investigated longer-term effects of CBT, finding there were large effect sizes for the reduction of depressive symptoms with CBT in the short-term, but there were no differences between CBT therapies and TAU in the medium term. Yet Lopez-Lopez et al. (2019) do acknowledge they did not have enough studies reporting mid-term effects to draw accurate conclusions. Therefore, the effectiveness of CBT for MDD is well-documented in the literature with additional studies supporting this link (Lepping et al., 2020; NICE, 2022; Twomey et al., 2015) and we have mentioned how research finds CBT is more effective than other psychotherapies supporting its treatment dominance, see the number of times it is mentioned in NICE (2022) for evidence, but this review has already started to mention some potential drawbacks of the CBT literature.

Furthermore, control groups are needed in research literature to know if the intervention is working and these effects can be separated from the effects of other interventions (Pithon, 2013). Therefore, a strength of the CBT literature is the strong emphasis on using control groups. For example, a multitude of studies use waiting-list controls and TAU groups. By using CBT and TAU groups, Mathiasen et al. (2016) found CBT was more effective than the TAU group, Olatunji et al. (2010) found CBT was more effective than placebo and waiting-list control groups and this was supported by additional studies (Carpenter et al., 2018; Norton et al., 2007). These findings are supported by the CBT literature's extensive use of Randomised Controlled Trials too in several studies (David et al., 2018; Manber et al., 2016; Mathiasen et al., 2016; Twomey et al., 2015) meaning the literature benefits from RCT methodology being the most empirical and robust methodology in establishing whether a cause-and-effect relationship exists (Bhide et al., 2018). Overall, control groups and RCTs allow CBT researchers to empirically support their claims about the effectiveness of CBT interventions and they can prove it is the CBT intervention itself reducing depressive symptoms, not the act of doing something and RCT allow researchers to know CBT causes a reduction in symptoms and not another third variable.

Another sign of CBT's effectiveness for MDD is evidenced in relapse rate research. Since the relapse rate of MDD after one depressive episode is 50%, after two episodes it is 80% and after three episodes it increases up to 90% (Katon et al., 2001; Kessing et al., 2004). Therefore, after each depressive episode, MDD gets worse and the risk of relapse increases (Belsher and Costello, 1988; Kendler et al., 2000). This is why relapse data is critical in evaluating CBT effectiveness especially as MDD relapse has a high cost to clients, society and families (Collins et al., 2011; Judd et al., 2000). As a result, Zhang et al. (2018) conducted a meta-analysis with 1945 participants across 16 trials finding CBT was the most effective treatment compared to control groups (like TAU, waiting lists, placebos and psychoeducation) by reducing relapse risk by 50% (Zhang et al., 2018). The meta-analysis found the relapse rate for MDD after 24 months compared to control groups was reduced by 76%. This finding is supported by Hollon et al. (2005) finding CBT had the lowest relapse rate at 31% after 12 months compared to medication (47%) and placebo control groups (76%). Hence, demonstrating the effectiveness of CBT at reducing depressive symptoms in the short-term and making sure symptoms do not return in the long term by equipping clients with the psychological tools and techniques required for living everyday life without their maladaptive coping mechanisms (Davey et al., 2015).

Additionally, National Institute for Health and Care Excellence (NICE) Guidelines are effective tools for this review to examine CBT since NICE Guidelines examine and consider all available research to create guidelines for practitioners (NICE, 2022) highlighting benefits and drawbacks to the therapy. For instance, for the guidelines to recommend CBT as an intervention means there is sufficient supporting research warranting the inclusion and NICE (2022) mentions how CBT helps clients avoid potential side effects of medications, how helpful it is for people who recognise they have unhelpful, negative and maladaptive thoughts and behavioural patterns they want to change, and (individual) CBT is effective for people who do not want to discuss their MDD in a group setting. Therefore, NICE (2022) highlights the benefits of CBT for MDD clients and these guidelines inform practitioners so they can effectively use CBT in real-life. This helps to support other research findings about the ecological validity of CBT in its real-world effectiveness (Otte, 2022) despite criticism of CBT research compromising ecological validity (Mathiasen et al., 2016).

However, NICE (2022) highlights drawbacks of CBT as well. Such as, individual CBT offers clients no opportunities to receive support from others with similar experiences and CBT depends on people being able to recognise their unhelpful, negative thought and behavioural patterns. Consequently, whilst these drawbacks could be fixed with Group CBT, allowing the client to meet others with shared experience if desired, NICE (2022) highlights how CBT might be considered the gold standard (David et al., 2018) but it is not without flaws as we will explore in the rest of this critical review.

In addition, longitudinal studies are desirable in research literatures because they help researchers understand the long-term effects of an intervention (Herdson et al., *under submission*) giving them a fuller understanding of how interventions work after clients leave the therapy room (Herdson et al., *under submission*). However, this review finds there is a lack of high-quality longitudinal research in CBT literature. For example, Quigley et al. (2018) claim to be a longitudinal analysis of cognitive change in CBT but the authors conclude their research supports the relationship between cognitive and symptom change but their research does not support a longitudinal relationship. Therefore, this study does not help researchers understand the long-term effects of CBT. Another example is Bernhardt et al. (2021) aiming to look at long-term effects of CBT in MDD but they did not use follow-ups and these researchers only investigated the effects of CBT whilst the participant was undergoing the treatment. This is useful as the literature understands how CBT leads to changes in a person's cognition during therapy, but it does not help researchers understand the effects of CBT 3-, 6- or 12 months after therapy ends. A final example is Rubin-Falcone et al. (2018) examining the neural effects of CBT, their results did not use follow-ups and this is another study focusing on the changes over a course of CBT. Overall, this review acknowledges the importance of understanding the workings of CBT over a course of treatment but CBT literature must use longer-term longitudinal studies addressing questions around the longer-term impacts of CBT since only a handful of studies do this currently like Hollon et al. (2005).

Building upon this, the CBT literature is negatively impacted by suboptimal research studies since Cuijpers et al. (2016) found the effect sizes of CBT are small-to-moderate in TAU or placebo groups compared to waiting list control groups, suggesting the large effect sizes found in CBT research could be overstated for three main reasons. Firstly, publication bias heavily impacts CBT literature (Cuijpers et al., 2010; Driessen et al., 2015) because journals require researchers to have strong findings (Dickersin, 1990) and Cuijpers et al. (2010) found there is indirect evidence of publication bias in psychotherapy research based on the excess publication of small studies with large effect sizes. Also, Dickersin (1990) found almost 25% of psychotherapy trials for adults with MDD are not published. Resulting in when the effect sizes of unpublished trials are added to published trials, the mean effect sizes decrease by more than 25% (Cuijpers et al., 2016). As a result, publication bias impacts the creditability of CBT research as research shows the effect sizes of CBT are overstated in published research meaning practitioners are being led to believe CBT is more effective than it might be in a real-world therapeutic setting. This is why greater steps should be taken within the academic community to counteract the effects of publication bias.

Secondly, many CBT trials are suboptimal with only 11 out of 115 trials meeting all basic indicators of quality and the effect sizes of these trials are significantly smaller than the sizes of lower-quality studies (Cuijpers et al., 2010), but there are methodological problems with Cuijpers et al. (2016) as they only included studies up to 2008 so it is unknown if newer studies are higher quality and nullify this criticism. Thirdly, the effect sizes of CBT research are overestimated when waiting lists are used as controls (Cuijpers et al., 2016), despite all control groups having their own problems (Cuijpers and Cristea, 2016; Mohr et al. 2009) because the waiting list control groups could be the opposite of a placebo and an inert treatment appearing to cause an adverse effect (Cuijpers et al., 2016) called a "nocebo" (Furukawa et al., 2014) and trials using this "control" overestimate the effects of CBT (Furukawa et al., 2014). Therefore, TAU and pill placebo groups allow researchers to better estimate the true effect size of CBT (Cuijpers et al., 2016). On the whole, despite Cuijpers et al. (2016)'s methodology issue of not including studies later than 2008 requiring this criticism to be researched further, CBT researchers should aim to design higher-quality studies using non-waiting-list control groups so practitioners can get a full understanding of the true effect size of CBT even if this results in the mean effect size decreasing, allowing them to provide better-informed treatment to their clients.

In conclusion, MDD can be treated by SSRIs restoring the chemical imbalance in the brain (Moncrieff et al., 2022), MBCT (Kuyken et al., 2008) based on the cognitive vulnerability model (Segal et al., 2013) and CBT, a highly effective (Lopez-Lopez et al., 2019) and gold standard (NICE, 2022) treatment for MDD. CBT is effective because it has no side effects this review could find, has large effect sizes (Lopez-Lopez et al., 2019) so researchers know CBT works for reducing MDD symptoms, and CBT is more effective than control groups (Whiston et al. (2019) and effective use of control groups in the literature is another strength, as seen in Mathiasen et al. (2016) and Olatunji et al. (2010) and RCT (David et al., 2018) so researchers know CBT is more effective and has lower relapse rates than other treatment options (Hollon et al., 2005; Zhang et al., 2018). Hence, researchers know CBT is the best treatment option to reduce the chance of MDD returning to clinically significant levels in clients. However, there are several issues with CBT and its literature like the lack of high-quality longitudinal studies so researchers cannot empirically support claims about CBT's long-term effectiveness, its use of suboptimal research practices (Cuijpers et al., 2016) because they overestimate the mean effect sizes of CBT when using waiting-list controls (Cuijpers et al., 2016) and publication bias inhibits researchers fully understanding the true mean effect size of CBT. Therefore, whilst this critical review concludes CBT is a highly effective MDD treatment because of its numerous advantages as discussed, we cannot state CBT is perfect and there are still several questions and issues about CBT and its literature that must be addressed moving forward.

REFERENCES

Albert, P. R., Benkelfat, C., & Descarries, L. (2012). The neurobiology of depression—revisiting the serotonin hypothesis. I. Cellular and molecular mechanisms. *Philosophical Transactions of the royal society B: Biological Sciences*, *367*(1601), 2378-2381.

Alloy, L. B., Abramson, L. Y., & Francis, E. L. (1999). Do negative cognitive styles confer vulnerability to depression?. *Current Directions in Psychological Science*, *8*(4), 128-132.

American Psychiatric Association. (2013). Diagnostic and statistical manual of mental disorders (5th ed.). https://doi.org/10.1176/appi.books.9780890425596.

Amidfar, M., Colic, L., Walter, M., & Kim, Y. K. (2018). Biomarkers of major depression related to serotonin receptors. *Current Psychiatry Reviews*, *14*(4), 239-244.

APA (2021) *What is Psychiatry?*. https://www.psychiatry.org/patients-families/what-is-psychiatry-menu. Accessed February 20, 2023.

Apolinário-Hagen, J., Drüge, M., & Fritsche, L. (2020). Cognitive behavioral therapy, mindfulness-based cognitive therapy and acceptance commitment therapy for anxiety disorders: integrating traditional with digital treatment approaches. *Anxiety Disorders: Rethinking and Understanding Recent Discoveries*, 291-329.

Bains, N., & Abdijadid, S. (2022). Major depressive disorder. In *StatPearls [Internet]*. StatPearls Publishing.

Beck, A. T., Hollon, S. D., Young, J. E., Bedrosian, R. C., & Budenz, D. (1985). Treatment of depression with cognitive therapy and amitriptyline. *Archives Of General Psychiatry, 42*(2), 142-148.

Belsher, G., & Costello, C. G. (1988). Relapse after recovery from unipolar depression: a critical review. *Psychological Bulletin, 104*(1), 84.

Bernhardt, M., Schwert, C., Aschenbrenner, S., Weisbrod, M., & Schröder, A. (2021). Longitudinal changes of cognitive deficits and treatment outcome of cognitive behavioral therapy for major depression. *The Journal of Nervous and Mental Disease, 209*(5), 336-342.

Bhide, A., Shah, P. S., & Acharya, G. (2018). A simplified guide to randomized controlled trials. *Acta Obstetricia Et Gynecologica Scandinavica, 97*(4), 380–387. https://doi.org/10.1111/aogs.13309

Carpenter, J. K., Andrews, L. A., Witcraft, S. M., Powers, M. B., Smits, J. A., & Hofmann, S. G. (2018). Cognitive behavioral therapy for anxiety and related disorders: A meta-analysis of randomized placebo-controlled trials. *Depression And Anxiety, 35*(6), 502-514.

Cascade, E., Kalali, A. H., & Kennedy, S. H. (2009). Real-world data on SSRI antidepressant side effects. *Psychiatry (Edgmont), 6*(2), 16.

Caspi, A., Sugden, K., Moffitt, T. E., Taylor, A., Craig, I. W., Harrington, H., ... & Poulton, R. (2003). Influence of life stress on depression: moderation by a polymorphism in the 5-HTT gene. *Science*, *301*(5631), 386-389.

Chassin, L., Beltran, I., Lee, M., Haller, M., & Villalta, I. (2010). Vulnerability to substance use disorders in childhood and adolescence.

Collins, P. Y., Patel, V., Joestl, S. S., March, D., Insel, T. R., Daar, A. S., ... & Walport, M. (2011). Grand challenges in global mental health. *Nature*, *475*(7354), 27-30.

Coppen, A. (1967). The biochemistry of affective disorders. *The British Journal of Psychiatry*, *113*(504), 1237-1264.

Cowen, P. J., & Browning, M. (2015). What has serotonin to do with depression?. *World Psychiatry*, *14*(2), 158.

Crane, C., Winder, R., Hargus, E., Amarasinghe, M., & Barnhofer, T. (2012). Effects of mindfulness-based cognitive therapy on specificity of life goals. *Cognitive Therapy And Research*, *36*, 182-189.

Cuijpers, P., & Cristea, I. A. (2016). How to prove that your therapy is effective, even when it is not: A guideline. *Epidemiology and Psychiatric Sciences*, 25 (5), 428–435.

Cuijpers, P., Cristea, I. A., Karyotaki, E., Reijnders, M., & Huibers, M. J. (2016). How effective are cognitive behavior therapies for major depression and anxiety disorders? A meta-analytic update of the evidence. *World Psychiatry*, *15*(3), 245-258.

Cuijpers, P., Smit, F., Bohlmeijer, E., Hollon, S. D., & Andersson, G. (2010). Efficacy of cognitive–behavioural therapy and other psychological treatments for adult depression: meta-analytic study of publication bias. *The British Journal of Psychiatry, 196*(3), 173-178.

Cuijpers, P., van Straten, A., Bohlmeijer, E., Hollon, S. D., & Andersson, G. (2010). The effects of psychotherapy for adult depression are overestimated: a meta-analysis of study quality and effect size. *Psychological Medicine, 40*(2), 211-223.

Davey, G., Lake, N., & Whittington, A. (Eds.). (2015). *Clinical Psychology*. Routledge.

David, D., Cristea, I., & Hofmann, S. G. (2018). Why cognitive behavioral therapy is the current gold standard of psychotherapy. *Frontiers In Psychiatry*, 4.

Dickersin, K. (1990). The existence of publication bias and risk factors for its occurrence. *Jama, 263*(10), 1385-1389.

Driessen, E., Hollon, S. D., Bockting, C. L., Cuijpers, P., & Turner, E. H. (2015). Does publication bias inflate the apparent efficacy of psychological treatment for major depressive disorder? A systematic review and meta-analysis of US National Institutes of Health-funded trials. *PloS One, 10*(9), e0137864.

Fenn, K., & Byrne, M. (2013). The key principles of cognitive behavioural therapy. *InnovAiT, 6*(9), 579-585.

Furukawa, T. A., Noma, H., Caldwell, D. M., Honyashiki, M., Shinohara, K., Imai, H., ... & Churchill, R. (2014). Waiting list may be a nocebo condition in psychotherapy trials: A contribution from network meta-analysis. *Acta Psychiatrica Scandinavica, 130*(3), 181-192.

Geddes, J. R., & Andreasen, N. C. (2020). *New Oxford Textbook Of Psychiatry*. Oxford University Press, USA.

GlaxoSmithKline (2009). *Paxil XR*. www.Paxilcr.com (site no longer available). Last accessed 27th Jan 2009.

Hahn, A., Haeusler, D., Kraus, C., Höflich, A. S., Kranz, G. S., Baldinger, P., ... & Lanzenberger, R. (2014). Attenuated serotonin transporter association between dorsal raphe and ventral striatum in major depression. *Human Brain Mapping, 35*(8), 3857-3866.

Harmer, C. J., Duman, R. S., & Cowen, P. J. (2017). How do antidepressants work? New perspectives for refining future treatment approaches. *The Lancet Psychiatry, 4*(5), 409-418.

Harrington, R. (2001). Depression, suicide and deliberate self-harm in adolescence. *British medical Bulletin, 57*(1), 47-60.

Healy, D. (2015). Serotonin and depression. *Bmj, 350*.

Herdson, O., Whiteley, C., Lashgari, E., Razzaghi, M., & Javadi, A. (2022) Working Towards Sampling and Methodological Guidelines for ASD Gamification Interventions: A Systematic Review. (Manuscript Submitted For Publication).

Hodo, D. W. (2006). Kaplan and Sadock's comprehensive textbook of psychiatry. *American Journal of Psychiatry, 163*(8), 1458-1458.

Hollon, S. D., DeRubeis, R. J., Shelton, R. C., Amsterdam, J. D., Salomon, R. M., O'Reardon, J. P., ... & Gallop, R. (2005). Prevention of relapse following cognitive therapy vs medications in moderate to severe depression. *Archives Of General Psychiatry, 62*(4), 417-422.

Jane Costello, E., Erkanli, A., & Angold, A. (2006). Is there an epidemic of child or adolescent depression?. *Journal Of Child Psychology And*

Psychiatry, 47(12), 1263-1271.

Judd, L. L., Akiskal, H. S., Zeller, P. J., Paulus, M., Leon, A. C., Maser, J. D., ... & Keller, M. B. (2000). Psychosocial disability during the long-term course of unipolar major depressive disorder. *Archives of General Psychiatry, 57*(4), 375-380.

Katon, W., Rutter, C., Ludman, E. J., Von Korff, M., Lin, E., Simon, G., ... & Unützer, J. (2001). A randomized trial of relapse prevention of depression in primary care. *Archives Of General Psychiatry, 58*(3), 241-247.

Kelly, K., Posternak, M., & Jonathan, E. A. (2022). Toward achieving optimal response: understanding and managing antidepressant side effects. *Dialogues In Clinical Neuroscience*.

Kendler, K. S., Thornton, L. M., & Gardner, C. O. (2000). Stressful life events and previous episodes in the etiology of major depression in women: an evaluation of the "kindling" hypothesis. *American Journal of Psychiatry, 157*(8), 1243-1251.

Kessing, L. V., Hansen, M. G., Andersen, P. K., & Angst, J. (2004). The predictive effect of episodes on the risk of recurrence in depressive and bipolar disorders—a life-long perspective. *Acta Psychiatrica Scandinavica, 109*(5), 339-344.

Knouse, L. E., & Ramsay, J. R. (2018). Managing side effects in CBT for adult ADHD. *The ADHD Report, 26*(2), 6-10.

Lepping, P., Whittington, R., Sambhi, R. S., Lane, S., Poole, R., Leucht, S., ... & Waheed, W. (2017). Clinical relevance of findings in trials of CBT for depression. *European Psychiatry, 45*, 207-211.

Lilly, E. (2006) *Prozac - How it works.* www.prozac.com/how_prozac/how_it_works.j

sp?reqNavId=2.2. (site no longer available). Last accessed 10th Feb 2006.

López-López, J. A., Davies, S. R., Caldwell, D. M., Churchill, R., Peters, T. J., Tallon, D., ... & Welton, N. J. (2019). The process and delivery of CBT for depression in adults: a systematic review and network meta-analysis. *Psychological Medicine*, *49*(12), 1937-1947.

Ma, S. H., & Teasdale, J. D. (2004). Mindfulness-based cognitive therapy for depression: replication and exploration of differential relapse prevention effects. *Journal Of Consulting And Clinical Psychology*, *72*(1), 31.

Manber, R., Buysse, D. J., Edinger, J., Krystal, A., Luther, J. F., Wisniewski, S. R., ... & Thase, M. E. (2016). Efficacy of cognitive-behavioral therapy for insomnia combined with antidepressant pharmacotherapy in patients with comorbid depression and insomnia: a randomized controlled trial. *The Journal Of Clinical Psychiatry*, *77*(10), 2446.

Mathiasen, K., Andersen, T. E., Riper, H., Kleiboer, A. A., & Roessler, K. K. (2016). Blended CBT versus face-to-face CBT: a randomised non-inferiority trial. *BMC Psychiatry*, *16*(1), 1-8.

Mohr, D. C., Spring, B., Freedland, K. E., Beckner, V., Arean, P., Hollon, S. D., ... & Kaplan, R. (2009). The selection and design of control conditions for randomized controlled trials of psychological interventions. *Psychotherapy And Psychosomatics*, *78*(5), 275-284.

Moncrieff, J., Cooper, R. E., Stockmann, T., Amendola, S., Hengartner, M. P., & Horowitz, M. A. (2022). The serotonin theory of depression: a systematic umbrella review of the evidence. *Molecular*

Psychiatry, 1-14.

National Institute for Clinical Excellence. (2018). Depression in adults: treatment and management. *NICE Guideline: Short Version Draft for Second Consultation.*

Norton, P. J., & Price, E. C. (2007). A meta-analytic review of adult cognitive-behavioral treatment outcome across the anxiety disorders. *The Journal Of Nervous And Mental Disease*, *195*(6), 521-531.

Olatunji, B. O., Cisler, J. M., & Deacon, B. J. (2010). Efficacy of cognitive behavioral therapy for anxiety disorders: a review of meta-analytic findings. *Psychiatric Clinics*, *33*(3), 557-577.

Otte, C. (2022). Cognitive behavioral therapy in anxiety disorders: current state of the evidence. *Dialogues In Clinical Neuroscience*.

Oud, M., De Winter, L., Vermeulen-Smit, E., Bodden, D., Nauta, M., Stone, L., ... & Stikkelbroek, Y. (2019). Effectiveness of CBT for children and adolescents with depression: A systematic review and meta-regression analysis. *European Psychiatry*, *57*, 33-45.

Pescosolido, B. A., Martin, J. K., Long, J. S., Medina, T. R., Phelan, J. C., & Link, B. G. (2010). "A disease like any other"? A decade of change in public reactions to schizophrenia, depression, and alcohol dependence. *American Journal of Psychiatry*, *167*(11), 1321-1330.

Pies, R. (2011) *Psychiatry's New Brain-Mind and the Legend of the "Chemical Imbalance.".* https://www.psychiatrictimes.com/view/psychiatrys-new-brain-mind-and-legend-chemical-imbalance. Accessed February 20, 2023.

Pilkington, P. D., Reavley, N. J., & Jorm, A. F. (2013). The Australian public's beliefs about the causes of depression: Associated factors and changes over 16 years. *Journal of Affective Disorders*, *150*(2), 356-362.

Pithon, M. M. (2013). Importance of the control group in scientific research. Dental Press Journal of Orthodontics, 18(6), 13-14.

Quigley, L., Dozois, D. J., Bagby, R. M., Lobo, D. S., Ravindran, L., & Quilty, L. C. (2019). Cognitive change in cognitive-behavioural therapy v. pharmacotherapy for adult depression: a longitudinal mediation analysis. *Psychological Medicine*, *49*(15), 2626-2634.

Rubin-Falcone, H., Weber, J., Kishon, R., Ochsner, K., Delaparte, L., Doré, B., ... & Miller, J. M. (2018). Longitudinal effects of cognitive behavioral therapy for depression on the neural correlates of emotion regulation. *Psychiatry Research: Neuroimaging*, *271*, 82-90.

Segal, Z., Williams, M., & Teasdale, J. (2018). *Mindfulness-based cognitive therapy for depression*. Guilford Publications.

Sipe, W. E., & Eisendrath, S. J. (2012). Mindfulness-based cognitive therapy: theory and practice. *The Canadian Journal of Psychiatry*, *57*(2), 63-69.

Smit, H. F. E., Bohlmeijer, E. T., Cuijpers, W. J. M. J., & Beekman, A. T. F. (2003). *Wetenschappelijke onderbouwing depressiepreventie: epidemiologie, aangrijpingspunten, huidige praktijk, nieuwe richtingen*. Trimbos-instituut.

Teasdale, J. D., Moore, R. G., Hayhurst, H., Pope, M., Williams, S., & Segal, Z. V. (2002). Metacognitive awareness and prevention of relapse in depression: empirical evidence. *Journal Of Consulting And Clinical Psychology*, *70*(2), 275.

Teasdale, J. D., Segal, Z. V., Williams, J. M. G., Ridgeway, V. A., Soulsby, J. M., & Lau, M. A. (2000). Prevention of relapse/recurrence in major depression by mindfulness-based cognitive therapy. *Journal Of Consulting And Clinical Psychology*, *68*(4), 615.

Thapar, A., Collishaw, S., Pine, D. S., & Thapar, A. K. (2012). Depression in adolescence. *The Lancet*, *379*(9820), 1056-1067.

Twomey, C., O'Reilly, G., & Byrne, M. (2015). Effectiveness of cognitive behavioural therapy for anxiety and depression in primary care: a meta-analysis. *Family Practice*, *32*(1), 3-15.

van der Velden, A. M., Kuyken, W., Wattar, U., Crane, C., Pallesen, K. J., Dahlgaard, J., ... & Piet, J. (2015). A systematic review of mechanisms of change in mindfulness-based cognitive therapy in the treatment of recurrent major depressive disorder. *Clinical Psychology Review*, *37*, 26-39.

Wang, S. M., Han, C., Bahk, W. M., Lee, S. J., Patkar, A. A., Masand, P. S., & Pae, C. U. (2018). Addressing the side effects of contemporary antidepressant drugs: a comprehensive review. *Chonnam Medical Journal*, *54*(2), 101-112.

Whiston, A., Bockting, C. L., & Semkovska, M. (2019). Towards personalising treatment: a systematic review and meta-analysis of face-to-face efficacy moderators of cognitive-behavioral therapy and interpersonal psychotherapy for major depressive disorder. *Psychological Medicine*, *49*(16), 2657-2668.

Yohn, C. N., Gergues, M. M., & Samuels, B. A. (2017). The role of 5-HT receptors in depression. *Molecular Brain*, *10*(1), 1-12.

Zhang, Z., Zhang, L., Zhang, G., Jin, J., & Zheng, Z. (2018). The effect of CBT and its modifications for relapse prevention in major depressive disorder: a systematic review and meta-analysis. *BMC Psychiatry*, *18*, 1-14.

Brown, J., Scholle, H. S., Azur, M. (2014). Strategies for measuring the quality of psychotherapy: A white paper to inform measure development and implementation. U.S. Department of Health and Human Services Assistant Secretary for Planning and Evaluation Office of Disability, Aging and Long-Term Care Policy. (ASPE)

Wampold, E. B. (2015). How important are the common factors in psychotherapy? An update. World Psychiatry, 14, 270-277. https://doi.org/10.1002/wps.20238

Understanding psychotherapy and how it works. (2012, November 1). American Psychological Association. Retrieved November 4, 2022 from https://www.apa.org/topics /psychotherapy/understanding

Carr, A. & McNulty, M. (Eds.) (2016). *The Handbook of Adult Clinical Psychology: An Evidence-Based Approach* (2nd Ed.) Hove: Routledge. Chapter 9.

Davey, G. (2014). *Psychopathology: Research, Assessment and Treatment in Clinical Psychology* (2nd Ed.). Chichester: Wiley. Chapter 7.

Kennerley, H., Kirk, J. & Westbrook, D. (2016). *An Introduction to cognitive behaviour therapy: skills and applications* (3rd Ed.). London: Sage. Chapters 1-11 (CBT approaches & techniques); Chapter 12 (Depression).

Ciharova, M., Furukawa, T. A., Efthimiou, O., Karyotaki, E., Miguel, C., Noma, H., Cipriani, A., Riper, H., & Cuijpers, P. (2021). Cognitive restructuring, behavioral activation and cognitive-behavioral therapy in the treatment of adult depression: A network meta-analysis. *Journal of consulting and clinical psychology*, *89*(6), 563–574. https://doi.org/10.1037/ccp0000654

https://www.subscribepage.com/psychologyboxset

CHECK OUT THE PSYCHOLOGY WORLD PODCAST FOR MORE PSYCHOLOGY INFORMATION! AVAILABLE ON ALL MAJOR PODCAST APPS.

About the author:

Connor Whiteley is the author of over 60 books in the sci-fi fantasy, nonfiction psychology and books for writer's genre and he is a Human Branding Speaker and Consultant.

He is a passionate warhammer 40,000 reader, psychology student and author.

Who narrates his own audiobooks and he hosts The Psychology World Podcast.

All whilst studying Psychology at the University of Kent, England.

Also, he was a former Explorer Scout where he gave a speech to the Maltese President in August 2018 and he attended Prince Charles' 70th Birthday Party at Buckingham Palace in May 2018.

Plus, he is a self-confessed coffee lover!

All books in 'An Introductory Series':
Careers In Psychology
Psychology of Suicide
Dementia Psychology
Clinical Psychology Reflections Volume 4
Forensic Psychology of Terrorism And Hostage-Taking
Forensic Psychology of False Allegations
Year In Psychology
CBT For Anxiety
CBT For Depression
Applied Psychology
BIOLOGICAL PSYCHOLOGY 3RD EDITION
COGNITIVE PSYCHOLOGY THIRD EDITION
SOCIAL PSYCHOLOGY- 3RD EDITION
ABNORMAL PSYCHOLOGY 3RD EDITION
PSYCHOLOGY OF RELATIONSHIPS- 3RD EDITION
DEVELOPMENTAL PSYCHOLOGY 3RD EDITION
HEALTH PSYCHOLOGY
RESEARCH IN PSYCHOLOGY
A GUIDE TO MENTAL HEALTH AND TREATMENT AROUND THE WORLD-

A GLOBAL LOOK AT DEPRESSION
FORENSIC PSYCHOLOGY
THE FORENSIC PSYCHOLOGY OF THEFT, BURGLARY AND OTHER CRIMES AGAINST PROPERTY
CRIMINAL PROFILING: A FORENSIC PSYCHOLOGY GUIDE TO FBI PROFILING AND GEOGRAPHICAL AND STATISTICAL PROFILING.
CLINICAL PSYCHOLOGY
FORMULATION IN PSYCHOTHERAPY
PERSONALITY PSYCHOLOGY AND INDIVIDUAL DIFFERENCES
CLINICAL PSYCHOLOGY REFLECTIONS VOLUME 1
CLINICAL PSYCHOLOGY REFLECTIONS VOLUME 2
Clinical Psychology Reflections Volume 3
CULT PSYCHOLOGY
Police Psychology

A Psychology Student's Guide To University
How Does University Work?
A Student's Guide To University And Learning
University Mental Health and Mindset

Other books by Connor Whiteley:

Bettie English Private Eye Series

A Very Private Woman

The Russian Case

A Very Urgent Matter

A Case Most Personal

Trains, Scots and Private Eyes

The Federation Protects

Lord of War Origin Trilogy:

Not Scared Of The Dark

Madness

Burn Them All

The Fireheart Fantasy Series

Heart of Fire

Heart of Lies

Heart of Prophecy

Heart of Bones

Heart of Fate

City of Assassins (Urban Fantasy)

City of Death

City of Marytrs

City of Pleasure

City of Power

<u>Agents of The Emperor</u>
Return of The Ancient Ones
Vigilance
Angels of Fire
Kingmaker
The Eight
The Lost Generation
Hunt
Emperor's Council
Speaker of Treachery
Birth Of The Empire
Terraforma

<u>The Rising Augusta Fantasy Adventure Series</u>
Rise To Power
Rising Walls
Rising Force
Rising Realm

<u>Lord Of War Trilogy (Agents of The Emperor)</u>
Not Scared Of The Dark
Madness
Burn It All Down

Gay Romance Novellas
Breaking, Nursing, Repairing A Broken Heart
Jacob And Daniel
Fallen For A Lie
Spying And Weddings

The Garro Series- Fantasy/Sci-fi
GARRO: GALAXY'S END
GARRO: RISE OF THE ORDER
GARRO: END TIMES
GARRO: SHORT STORIES
GARRO: COLLECTION
GARRO: HERESY
GARRO: FAITHLESS
GARRO: DESTROYER OF WORLDS
GARRO: COLLECTIONS BOOK 4-6
GARRO: MISTRESS OF BLOOD
GARRO: BEACON OF HOPE
GARRO: END OF DAYS

Winter Series- Fantasy Trilogy Books
WINTER'S COMING
WINTER'S HUNT
WINTER'S REVENGE
WINTER'S DISSENSION

<u>Miscellaneous:</u>
RETURN
FREEDOM
SALVATION
Reflection of Mount Flame
The Masked One
The Great Deer
English Independence

OTHER SHORT STORIES BY CONNOR WHITELEY

<u>Mystery Short Story Collections</u>
Criminally Good Stories Volume 1: 20 Detective Mystery Short Stories
Criminally Good Stories Volume 2: 20 Private Investigator Short Stories
Criminally Good Stories Volume 3: 20 Crime Fiction Short Stories
Criminally Good Stories Volume 4: 20 Science Fiction and Fantasy Mystery Short Stories
Criminally Good Stories Volume 5: 20 Romantic Suspense Short Stories

Mystery Short Stories:
Protecting The Woman She Hated
Finding A Royal Friend
Our Woman In Paris
Corrupt Driving
A Prime Assassination
Jubilee Thief
Jubilee, Terror, Celebrations
Negative Jubilation
Ghostly Jubilation
Killing For Womenkind
A Snowy Death
Miracle Of Death
A Spy In Rome
The 12:30 To St Pancras
A Country In Trouble
A Smokey Way To Go
A Spicy Way To GO
A Marketing Way To Go
A Missing Way To Go
A Showering Way To Go
Poison In The Candy Cane
Christmas Innocence
You Better Watch Out
Christmas Theft
Trouble In Christmas
Smell of The Lake

Problem In A Car
Theft, Past and Team
Embezzler In The Room
A Strange Way To Go
A Horrible Way To Go
Ann Awful Way To Go
An Old Way To Go
A Fishy Way To Go
A Pointy Way To Go
A High Way To Go
A Fiery Way To Go
A Glassy Way To Go
A Chocolatey Way To Go
Kendra Detective Mystery Collection Volume 1
Kendra Detective Mystery Collection Volume 2
Stealing A Chance At Freedom
Glassblowing and Death
Theft of Independence
Cookie Thief
Marble Thief
Book Thief
Art Thief
Mated At The Morgue
The Big Five Whoopee Moments
Stealing An Election

Mystery Short Story Collection Volume 1
Mystery Short Story Collection Volume 2
Criminal Performance
Candy Detectives
Key To Birth In The Past

<u>Science Fiction Short Stories:</u>
Temptation
Superhuman Autospy
Blood In The Redwater
All Is Dust
Vigil
Emperor Forgive Us
Their Brave New World
Gummy Bear Detective
The Candy Detective
What Candies Fear
The Blurred Image
Shattered Legions
The First Rememberer
Life of A Rememberer
System of Wonder
Lifesaver
Remarkable Way She Died
The Interrogation of Annabella Stormic
Blade of The Emperor
Arbiter's Truth

Computation of Battle
Old One's Wrath
Puppets and Masters
Ship of Plague
Interrogation
Edge of Failure
One Way Choice
Acceptable Losses
Balance of Power
Good Idea At The Time
Escape Plan
Escape In The Hesitation
Inspiration In Need
Singing Warriors
Knowledge is Power
Killer of Polluters
Climate of Death
The Family Mailing Affair
Defining Criminality
The Martian Affair
A Cheating Affair
The Little Café Affair
Mountain of Death
Prisoner's Fight
Claws of Death
Bitter Air
Honey Hunt

Blade On A Train
<u>Fantasy Short Stories:</u>
City of Snow
City of Light
City of Vengeance
Dragons, Goats and Kingdom
Smog The Pathetic Dragon
Don't Go In The Shed
The Tomato Saver
The Remarkable Way She Died
The Bloodied Rose
Asmodia's Wrath
Heart of A Killer
Emissary of Blood
Dragon Coins
Dragon Tea
Dragon Rider
Sacrifice of the Soul
Heart of The Flesheater
Heart of The Regent
Heart of The Standing
Feline of The Lost
Heart of The Story
City of Fire
Awaiting Death

www.ingramcontent.com/pod-product-compliance
Lightning Source LLC
LaVergne TN
LVHW012112070526
838202LV00056B/5705